BIRD'S CUSTARD ISLAND

BIRD'S CUSTARD ISLAND

A Culinary Memoir

Lucia Adams

To order additional copies of this book, contact:
Xlibris Corporation
1-888-795-4274
www.Xlibris.com
Orders@Xlibris.com
39943

CONTENTS

DEDICATION

In Memory of my Brother Donny

Bird's Custard Island

The great art critic Roger Fry called England *Bird's Custard Island*, with not-so-veiled snobbery at the culinary habits of the unaesthetic classes. The yellow custard powder, one of the New Age's first fast foods, bolstered the troops in both world wars and is still very much in evidence on English pantry shelves. Ironically Fry's own industrious Quaker family had mass-produced the first convenience staple, the chocolate bar, in 1847.

In Kendal's Palladian Abbot Hall, in the foothills of the high fells of the Lake District, one rain swept night I lectured about Fry's paintings, which he always took far more seriously than his writing. After an hour of respectful silence a hand shot up and a county woman in Ribchester tweeds wondered about the 1918 painting of the chocolate cake. She cared not about Cubist or whatever those influences were supposed to be but where do you think he got all that the chocolate during the War? The room came to life, eyes brightened, opinions abounded, recipes and memories shared and Post-Impressionism soon forgotten.

Judging from Virginia Woolf's biography of Fry and his letters and papers he could have cared a fig for food in England, eating quickly amongst the palettes and paint fumes, creating life-long stomach problems for which he sought crank cures. He had of course also endured nursery stodge and public school starvation that his friends Bertrand Russell and Kenneth Clark recounted in their memoirs. Then he discovered France! And Freedom! And everything changed! He painted in Brantome, St. Remy, Les Baux, amidst aromatic markets, fragrant riverbanks, eating pears, pates, and rapturous cheeses. In the South of France he was always, as Woolf remarks, "in the succulent valleys, living".

In *A Room of One's Own* she wrote," It is part of the novelist's convention not to mention soup and salmon and ducklings, as if soup and salmon and ducklings were of no importance." No Marmite, no HP Sauce, no fish and chips or Bird's Custard for this privileged society! Since English cooking was "an abomination" with its boiled cabbage and intractable meat, the upper classes had raided French cuisine since the Middle Ages. While Clive Bell dined at the Café Royal, Vanessa gave dinner orders to the cook to try that Provencal dish she had discovered during her trip with Roger Fry.

The colorful, rustic pottery Fry bought in Provence adorned the kitchen of his daughter, Pamela Diamand in her house, Bouchernes, in the seaside town of Maldon, Essex. I visited there many times to photograph Fry's paintings, which were covered with wax bread wrappers that Pamela's husband Micu printed in the adjacent garage. The beautiful slate blue house, which her father bought, resembled a French maison de campagne with a large tiled kitchen and airy rooms overlooking the garden. Here we had lunches, teas and dinners, all very austere and economical, though today one would just call them healthy. On the long refectory table was Bulmer's cider, the same bottle one saw on Lord Strickland's sideboard in Sizergh Castle and probably every other residential castle in the country. The meal was always a variation on the theme of vegetable soup (sometimes broth, sometimes heartier), followed by fried sprats or a communal slice of gammon and a salad.

Pamela also had a flat in Holland Park in London, inherited from her aunt Margery. While scouting out local Bloomsbury art collections or lunching with Alison Waley, the Orientalist Arthur's widow who was trying to find who had just stolen his papers, I stayed in a small paint-encrusted bedroom and ate the identical spare fare set out on a paint-encrusted dining room table, surrounded by walls festooned with paintings a la Matisse, a la Derain, a la Vlaminck and a la everyone else Fry and Vanessa Bell and Duncan Grant and even Virginia copied.

PRINCETON FARE

Lee and I moved to Princeton in 1964 where he was a graduate student in the History Department. From the day we married cooking became a delectation and delight, curiously so since I had literally never even boiled an egg. My charming, light-hearted mother had banished me from the kitchen, and remembering her own Depression-era childhood just wanted me to be happy, creating a more subtle form of pressure.

The dining room on the top floor of the imposing doctor's house at 10 Bayard Lane was a public pronouncement that we, The Beiers, wanted the Best in Life and the culture of the table was to be its quintessential statement. No Woolworth plates for Us! Our table was set with Lenox, Georg Jensen, Daum coupes and goblets, and Belgian damask, which Lee bought during his Fulbright year in Nancy, France. Along with that 25 pound blue leather volume of Henri Pellaprat's *L'Art Culinaire Moderne,* which I never learned to decipher, just cooking one dish, a labor intensive, sweet canard a l'orange. It was enough to put you off cooking for good!

Julia Child' s *Mastering the Art of French Cooking* had, however, arrived at the perfect time. I studied it, page by page, like the Bible and soon felt equipped to cook what I thought was haute cuisine, but which was really *la cuisine bourgeoise* according to Mme. Saint-Ange. For our very first dinner party, for a faculty member, in this stratified society a very bold move, (President and Mrs. Robert Goheen had other plans that night) I made vichyssoise, steak with Béarnaise, pommes de terre Anna and a cherry clafouti. The soup was gritty, the sauce yellow and curdled, the steak like Wellington's boots and I soon learned that good cooking is about methodology and preparation, despite today's mantra ingredients—ingredients—ingredients.

At the time American cooking was largely Anglo-Saxon, meaning meat and potatoes and 'another vegetable' every night. Native ingredients like corn or pumpkins or clams and a new interest in multi-culturalism were slowly creating a vernacular cuisine but at the time we had to make do with what James Beard called "overtones" of Italian, German, Chinese, Hawaiian cooking. In 1964 overtones of Italian meant spaghetti with meat sauce, that combination of ground beef, onions, green peppers, mushrooms, a handful of dried oregano and tomato sauce, cooked for three hours and served on Friday nights with garlic bread and iceberg lettuce. And who can forget those "French" fondue pots on capricious Sterno burners soon to be discarded as we searched the Seven Seas for authentic alternatives.

Today when I see a copy of the first edition of *Mastering* I get a pang for that time in life when every new recipe meant adventure and a vast culinary future stooped to be conquered. My favorite recipe of Julia's has always been Cocotte Bonne Femme which I have cooked repeatedly over the years because the ingredients are ubiquitous, bacon, potatoes, onions, a chicken, sprinkled with thyme and baked with a splash of white wine. I never followed Julia's recipes exactly and never duplicated the same results twice, nor did I take a shine to baking, lacking patience and wishing to blend many things together serendipitously. It was the identical penchant revealed in Comp Lit class when Professor Richard Vowles (the world's nicest man) admonished against haphazardly throwing together comparisons of Kierkegaard, Strindberg, Madame Blavatsky and the kitchen sink. Personality always emerges in the kitchen. Forget the shrinks; pick up a pot and The Real You will emerge.

The synergy between food and social life in Princeton was nowhere more evident that at a July 4th picnic in 1965 outside the World War II prefab of the Art Donovan's. Art had been my History of Science teacher in Madison, Wisconsin and it was in his class I first heard President Kennedy had been shot. He gave students the option to leave or stay and learn about stellar parallaxes. Such mystifying New England coolness! Two years later, from a long copper fish steamer emerged a beautiful pink poached salmon (my first time, now so common) adorned with pale green cucumber sauce served by his wife Margaret along with a witch's brew of invective about our objection to the Vietnam War. She said angrily, "Why don't you move to Russia if you don't like it here." Russia was then the equivalent of Hades.

In the end, like so many wives then she probably "sacrificed everything for her husband's career, entertaining those who needed impressing and cooking elaborate meals for those who needed feeding.", a resonating quote about Barbara Bush in a recent book. I know, I did the same. Over the years we had dozens and dozens and dozens of friends, colleagues and professors to dinner and I cooked elaborate meals for every single one, accepting merrily the three day commitment, one for planning and buying the provisions, one for cooking, and finally one for cleaning up. In retrospect I perhaps should have pursued the Ph.D not kudos for cooking given the vagaries of the workplace!

Nancy Starr, a classic-model graduate student wife, i.e. from a good family and possessing all the domestic arts along with proficiency on the cello, was married to Fred, James Billington's top graduate student. Like Art, he supported the war in Vietnam and being of Hungarian descent was passionately anti-Communist; he later became President of Oberlin College, though with his alarming brilliance and ambition we expected him to become Ambassador to Russia.

For one dinner we misread the social signals completely. Lee, a Rice Lake, Wisconsin boy whose alter ego was F. Scott Fitzgerald, dressed in a three-piece Brooks Brothers suit and I wore a cashmere Peck and Peck dress; we brought a bottle of French wine, only to find the Starrs and the

Friar Calhouns and the others in dungarees grilling hamburgers, drinking beer and watching baseball on the much dreaded TV.

Mon Dieu! We were shocked. There was no finesse in this simple dish: supermarket chopped meat (maybe chuck, maybe round, what's the difference?) plopped on an outdoor charcoal grill smelling of lighter fluid, charred a bit, thrown on a flimsy packaged bun too light to bear the weight of the meat, tomato, slab of onion, the iceberg, and hill of ketchup. Quite a mess on the paper plates! We were also served hotdogs which we would not touch since we had toured the Oscar Meyer plant.

At my very first job, copywriter at the ersatz publishing house Van Nostrand, I became friends with advertising chief Hugh Dennett in his patent leather pumps and Patricia Pogue undergoing a divorce from Seth, a wine merchant who amused us with stories of Arlene Dahl and Alexis Lichine who had never eaten alone during their four-year marriage. Not even once!

We three often lunched at The Princeton Inn and at this time in employment history you went to lunch at 1:30 or 2:00, ordered a martini or two, or a glass of that viscous Almaden red, mushrooms on toast, then returned to turn off the light at your desk. I tried these mushrooms at home, using Julia's béchamel, a dash of Dry Sack, dried herbs (in the era before fresh ones) two cans of sliced mushrooms, served over white toast.

For nightly dinners, at a time when everyone ate at home, the same dusty bottle of sherry, in its burlap shift, emerged to enhance chicken baked with cream of mushroom soup, topped with Swiss and served with Uncle Ben's. This recipe was as ubiquitous as tuna casserole with the same can of soup, frozen green peas, elbow macaroni, and Bumblebee, which looked and smelled like Jerome's catfood.

Our orange tabby was named after the head of the History Department, Jerome Blum, whom Patricia's guests pummeled one night with ice cubes during a game of Barbershop though I prefer to recall my first moussaka.

It was staggeringly delicious, the creamy eggplant, the meat sauce with a touch of cinnamon and the completely unexpected custard top. It beat eggplant Parmesan hands down!

PARIS AND FRANCE

In the Spring of 1966 we moved to Paris so Lee could explain—for once and for all—the causes of the French Revolution and where I embraced food with gusto, so much gusto that I quickly gained ten pounds from croissants, (the whole world would discover them in 10 years), apricot tarts, baguettes with butter and jam, more baguettes with jambon and Brie at lunch. For dinner it was stale baguettes at the subsidized student restaurants, Censier, Mabillion, Mazet, Le Petit Palais where for a few francs you could also eat chewy cheval, brains, tripe, watery yogurt and unripe fruit in the company of enraged North Vietnamese students who swarmed to our table to engager les americains. Then out into the cold, past the paniers de salade, the police paddy wagons always looking for recalcitrant students to throw in. Once they did when en route to the Opera to see *Tristan and Isolde* we found ourselves at a flag burning in the Place de la Concorde; stormed by leaded capes and batons, we never made the performance and I never went to another demonstration in the land of baguettes and Brie with a history of popular insurrection.

For my 24th birthday Lee made reservations at Lasserre, even more popular than Tour D'Argent. We were dumbstruck at the solemn, solicitous waiters, the solemn, church-like interior and the solemn prices on the menu. Should we flee? But wait, here's one and with no wine and l'eau fraiche we could manage! It's called Abattis de Volaille; little did we know that *abats* to a French butcher meant everything from heads to hearts to giblets and beyond, but, well, that must be chicken! Alors, the sad spectacle of bony chicken claws sticking straight up from a pale watery tomato grave with a lone sweetbread will always haunt me.

Ted Rex, then a Professor at Berkeley, was in town and asked us to be his guests at Allard's a beautiful bistro. Off we went on a rainy night to feast in golden light (why are American restaurants so poorly lit?) as in a La Tour painting. Ted was a new inductee into Academia, which he perceptively called the "tender trap", and a great host. The soigné waiter took our orders and recommended the special of the day, roast lamb with white haricot beans which I promptly ordered and which arrived pinkly glistening in a very garlicky au jus. (The French ate far more garlic than the Italians as you could tell from the phone booths).

Lee, seeing a more expensive item on the menu, opted for a roast duck with olives. There were two kinds, black and green, as we later saw strewn on Rue St. Andre des Arts along with the strawberries in Armagnac. Jason Epstein recently adapted this Allard's recipes in the *New York Times Magazine*. Stuff a duck with fresh thyme or rosemary and roast it for an hour, then pour in red wine, a mirepoix, lemon peel and bay leaves and roast it for another hour. Into the strained and reduced stock add green olives, maybe some black, add a tad of flour for a roux and voila Allard's Canard aux Olives.

Except for Jean Luc Godard and Daniel Cohn Bendit everyone in France loved Americans, and we took advantage of every moment of it, regular visiting dignitaries. Concierges vied to rent us apartments, one bribing us with a free, very old Vespa. On a freezing November day, even colder on the slow scooter, we rode across a flat wheaten plain in the Loire Valley to see Chartres rising like a majestic mountain in the distance. Grasping Henry Adams's *Mont Saint Michel and Chartres* while searching the nave, the clerestory and the stained glass for signs of that 13th century mystical unity, we quickly paid respects then dashed across the street for lunch.

Seated next to a bright fire in the stucco auberge and avoiding the thought of the freezing ride back to 120 Rue de Rennes, we drank Kir, ate garbure with pork, cabbage and carrots, and a soupcon of goose confit and plenty of bread. Magic. Imagination. Hopes of future cathedrals and garbures, of literature and stained glass and the whole world to see. I knew at the time it was a rare moment I would remember always. Here it is forty years later and I can still taste the soup-stew eaten in the shadow of the greatest cathedral in Europe.

On a visit to our friend Jean Paul Perrichi, in Arras in the Pas de Calais, we explored the tunnels under the city where the residents had escaped a half-century of Germans. We then mourned the dead in bombed out bunkers, with crushed helmets and rusted armaments, and paid respects in an ocean of white crosses. Treated like liberating heroes we were rewarded by the Perrichi with a feast, which included a fat bird cooked with leeks, local sausage and apples reflecting the Flemish influence on the city. Those with modest origins in France were abundantly gracious, and the table always groaned however small the apartments.

It was far different with the very stuffy family of Jean Claude Henri. In Dr. Henri's Parisian apartment next to the Jardin Des Plantes we were toasted by one glass of champagne, then had a decidedly not paysanne dinner of ripe cantaloupe filled with Port, and a large cold fish mousse served with tarragon mayonnaise and rissole potatoes. Madame Henri apologized for *les restes* and made it clear they did not normally drink, except on special occasions like this. They were not the likes of the Pericchi. Such fun it was observing national snobbisms and their infinite variations.

Jean Claude *fils* drove us some miles south of Strasbourg to visit Struthof-Natzweiler concentration camp in the haunting Vosges Mountains. Visitors were, at that time, permitted to enter the gas chamber on top of a snowy 3,000 foot high mountain, but I stayed outside in the cold air, throwing rocks on the ground, imagining escaping through the tall pines with yapping dogs at my heels. Later in the day I could not eat a bite in a grand Strasbourg restaurant. I was never to visit this capitol of gastronomy again, though in Chicago I have eaten Jean Joho's Alsatian country cuisine, geese, onion tarts. The region produces some of the best chefs in the world combining the finesse of French and the heft of German cuisine.

Bloomsbury and Cambridge

Fortified by French food, we moved across the channel to Cambridge, just when the Swinging Sixties supposedly got into gear. Lee decided to write his thesis about English poor relief under Lawrence Stone whose *Crisis of the Aristocracy* had just been published, hopefully settling that bitter score with Trevor-Roper and British academia. While collecting research for the thesis, we combed Warwickshire's county record offices and its gloomy, damp vicarages, for evidence of "sturdy beggars" and other misfits in 16th century England. History was after all about primary sources and "the people" and not just kings and queens.

Roger Fry had, luckily for me, deposited his papers and many large oil paintings in his alma mater, King's College. In its impressive wood paneled library I read his letters, lecture notes, autobiographical jottings, scattered in green solander boxes under the lascivious eye of bibliographer A.N.L. Munby. His aide de camp, a Mr. Loukes, was a tall weedy fellow without a university degree or proper accent, all of which created a scenario right from the Merchant-Ivory film *Remains of the Day*. Never were two Englishmen more separated by social class, the deferential and obsequious Loukes and Munby's haughty acceptance of his proper place in the Great Chain of Being. I tried to be extra polite to Loukes who probably thought I was a fool. Or just an American.

One day Quentin Bell, with his reddish beard and prominent eyes, strolled into the library to look at the papers of his art teacher, his mother's lover and his aunt Virginia's finest friend. After just a few minutes chat, he suggested we go for lunch at the college cafeteria. Presto! I would study at Leeds, where he was then Professor, and write a thesis about Fry's paintings. Never before nor since have I so wished that my father, who died the year before with Kenneth Clark's edition of Fry's *Last Lectures* on his lap, were still alive. Three years later, when I finished the thesis, the inquisition or viva, was a buffet in Bell's office with claret and Boursin and great conversation about how much he loved Roger Fry. This kind of savoir-faire could ruin you for life I thought, giving you a false view of the pettiness of academic life, and the harshness of working life in general. I searched in vain for such urbanity over the next ten years, but did become a Boursin addict, including it in scrambled eggs, salads or potato casseroles.

Some years later I invited Quentin Bell to help raise funds for the Ruskin Appeal Fund to save his last home, Brantwood, on the shores of Lake Coniston. Bell had never been to the Lake District, nor apparently had his father Clive ever been. He gave an obscure lecture called "James Burdon and John Ruskin" at Abbot Hall which was sparsely attended, the local gentry not having much intellectual curiosity as we noted previously. Anne Olivier Bell was as tall as her husband, as was Lee, but the four of us, piled into our tiny Morris Minor, driving over fell, moor and dale for the requisite visits to Rydal Mount and Dove Cottage and of course gloomy old Brantwood.

When asked where they would like to dine after the lecture they chose a pub, the Fleece, in Kendal with fine steak and kidney puddings and locally brewed bitters, and not Sharrow Bay, Miller Howe or Hodge Hill all fine restaurants in the Lake District. Steak and kidney pudding is fondly remembered by Colin Spencer in *British Food* to the point of emotionalism or as emotional as an Englishman can get. The best consists of finely chopped stewing steak like chuck or rump, a lamb's kidney, or if you are a classicist, ox kidney, maybe mushrooms, all steamed in a sturdy blanket of suet, that tasty fat surrounding cattles' kidneys, flour and milk. Steak and kidney pudding is infinitely more luscious than the baked short crust variety, or pie. I adore steamed food; there is nothing to get in the way of the essence of taste or texture.

Cambridge was startlingly lush with vegetation, and the garden of our narrow dark row house on De Freville Street was almost primeval with wild, overgrown mountains of blackberry (bramble) bushes which I made into countless pies, cobblers, crumbles, and fools, or threw into porridge or salads. Our cat, Bushy, whom we rescued on Garlic Row, had a white Elizabethan muff that seemed never to have regained its pristine color. There was no refrigerator, no central heating, plenty of chilblains, a walk-in pantry with potatoes, onions, maybe some anchovy paste or lime pickle, but I was more, much more, than happy to shop for perishables everyday. I was a born again zealot when discovering Sainsbury's. Nirvana! Gloriously different from the A&P in Princeton where the red Chevy station wagon was stocked weekly with Sara Lee frozen orange cake, frozen chopped meat, frozen Green Giant vegetables.

And so I became a linear shopper, a serial shopper, absolutely inexhaustible on my daily rounds, one stop at the meat counter, one perhaps at the fish, one at cheese, then the greengrocer, often the baker, the tea and coffee purveyor with the world's best Blue Mountain coffee beans stored in antique tin containers and roasted right there. I piled everything into the wicker basket of my bicycle as I pedaled home under a Constable sky across Midsummer Commons. After a morning reading letters and lectures or photographing Fry's paintings in Maynard Keynes' old digs I could not wait to hit the market. Market loitering is still my greatest leisure activity, aimlessly spending half a day looking at pomegranates or multi-colored eggplants and peppers, dead fish or hanging birds. Bliss.

HIGH TABLE AND LOW

Lee joined University College because it permitted wives to dine and there was no high table, a democratic gesture soon abandoned when he was invited to the old all male colleges. High table assumed that there should be a huge discrepancy between the fare of lowly students and high living, high thinking dons, as if by their food shall ye know them. No swans of St. John's at University College but stewed tomatoes strewn over a rubbery chop, watery potatoes and if lucky some Port and cheese.

While the men dined at those very high tables, Jeanne Stone, long past rage and disappointment, told me "the women stayed home and ate a hard boiled egg." She, the proud daughter of the French historian Fawtrier, had eaten many in her years, as Lawrence and Maurice Bowra and male visitors like Lee consumed Mouton-Rothschild and Chateaubriand at Wadham in a setting straight from C.P. Snow (*Corridors of Power* and *The Masters* were my favorite leisure reading at the time).

Virginia Woolf noted how dinners were so different in male and female colleges, while the men ate sumptuously the women had to do with bland, dreary foods. It didn't bother me particularly because I was so excited to be in Cambridge and we entertained and were entertained incessantly, always seeking a reincarnation of Bloomsbury wit and civility. The English were wildly more sociable, sophisticated and irreverent than the self-conscious academics at Princeton.

One evening we attended a wine tasting at University College conducted by Terrence "Wines" Zarratini one of those Cockneys of Italian extraction who possessed the dark Mediterranean looks and the self-consciously flamboyant personality to counterpoint the preternaturally reserved English. The wine was indifferent French but Terrence soon became inebriated and with a Bottoms Up Chaps bravura filled the tasting glasses to the brim opining "After a cooupla glasses it all tastes the same". I don't recall ever seriously challenging that opinion in my long history of wine drinking. When selling wine years later at Sherry-Lehmann in New York I found the common denominator for all the staff was quite simply—a love of drinking wine! As much as possible. At the time however this was the unwelcomed 'other side' of England, with Zarratinis appearing around every hedgerow while I communed with the spirits of the privileged class of fifty years before.

For our frequent soirees I served a repertoire of a few inexpensive hors d'oeuvres such as watercress or cucumber sandwiches on thin crustless white bread preciously cut into little triangles. There were plenty of "pots" or "pates" of fish, fowl and meats often served open-faced sandwich style since I had discovered the Penguin paperback on Danish Smorrebrod. Liver pate was liver sausage, softened butter, brandy or red wine, garlic, thyme blended together, put in a terrine and topped with a bay leaf. Smoked trout became pate when combined with cream cheese, a touch of mayo, lemon juice, and chives potted into antique Quimper. Presentation was always as important as contents as appreciative guests praised the Don Cortez Red at 10 shillings when poured from the Daum decanter into those fine Art Nouveau goblets.

Claudia Roden's Arab pizzas were also passed around to oohs and aahs. Basic pizza dough was topped with raw minced lamb or beef, tomato paste, allspice, fresh lemon juice and a bit of grated onion and baked till very brown. It is as good as Italian pizza. I lost my old paperback of *Middle Eastern Cooking* and today's fancy new version is unrecognizable with watered—down recipes for the contemporary cook, rather akin to Julia's popularizing tomes, making burgers with Jacques Pepin, a far cry from *Mastering*.

A perpetual guest, and upstairs flat mate was Russell Lawson, a Clare grad, who at 23 and a younger son in a strange land where primogeniture still existed, could not decide whether to be a bishop or go to Sandhurst; we never learned of his choice as we drank Benedictine and Brandy. "Oh no, I couldn't; you're much too generous, Oh well, all right if you insist" as the bottle was drained. The English loved nothing more than free spirits and viewed Americans as fair game for munificence because we after all did not understand the social code. Russell despised Prime Minister Harold Wilson. The unions ruined the country! A fierce Tory I am sure he must have been an ardent Thatcherite who although she was a greengrocer's daughter seemed to have had little love for the working poor. Social distinctions were so intense in England in 1967, and though historians insist this was a time of social change it did not seem that way to me.

RICHARD AND SARAH COCKE

We met Richard and Sarah Cocke at University College. Sarah Pollard's family was listed in *Debrett's Peerage* as her husband quickly pointed out. Very fair in all ways, physically and socially, Sarah was horrified by pretension. Go first class? How demeaning, such petty snobbery was strictly reserved for scrap metal merchants who drove Jaguars and not old Rovers. Her metier was photography, one of the few semi-professions acceptable to ladies, mainly undertaken to help Richard with his art historical needs, but her real job was cooking and entertaining since it was an absolute necessity for English wives to be accomplished, conscientious handmaidens to husbands on the ascent. Previous generations may have had cooks but not so in the 1960s.

Richard's mother, a war bride whose American husband abandoned her right after the baby's birth, also did her own cooking in her home in the Reitlinger Museum in Maidenhead where we spent one memorable Christmas amidst the majolica, rusted bathrooms and freezing bedrooms, causing quite a stir when we asked to take a bath. These Americans and their hygiene complex. After we steamed Harrods Christmas pudding and made hard sauce of butter and brandy, and before sitting down to the rib roast to be served in the somber museum that had recently been looted by antiques thieves, we took a hearty walk. When passing a pub Lee suggested popping in for a pint. The Cockes were aghast! They *never* had been to a pub and had no intention of doing so now. It was to be one of our greatest pleasures in the British Isles, no matter what county, popping in for a pint.

In Cambridge we were invited to dinner chez Cocke. Richard, in his *kuntsforschung* of the Baroque painter, Mola, wanted to impress Professors

Michael Jaffe and Francis Haskell. As so often I remember not the conversation but the menu, and have no idea if other people can remember what they had for dinner decades and decades ago. Here was the English Home Entertainment formula we experienced time and again for ten years: first arrive either exactly on time or at the absolute maximum ten minutes late, shake off your wet coats in the foyer, rub your hands vigorously before the fire, take your seat in the living room and accept a schooner of fino or amontillado. After just under half an hour head to the beautifully set table, take your designated seat, man, women, man, woman, hosts at the head and some light banter.

Colin Spencer writes that in the 1960s, "The middle classes socialized now by giving dinner parties, beginning inevitably with pork or chicken liver pates, followed by coq au vin." I howled when I read this. Spot on! Clear tinned consommé, a salmon quiche, or some combination of eggs and anchovies also preceded the ubiquitous coq, which we must have eaten at a hundred dinners in the coming years. Everything was served en famille helping oneself by passing around the cauliflower and red new potatoes sprinkled with parsley in Meissen bowls. I can never recall ever being served the main course already prepared on the plate, which was considered unbearably rude. It still irritates me when a hostess brings out a plate with the entire dinner on it, like a dog's bowl.

After the coq was the excellent rhubarb crumble. Like blackberries, rhubarb grew wild in every garden with big green shady leaves and seductive pink stems. A crumble of brown sugar and butter capped blanched rhubarb sweetened with sugar, lemon juice and a dash of vanilla, served with fresh, definitely not Bird's, custard. Custard is more delicious and versatile than whipped cream and is rarely explored outside of England though very simple to make; cornstarch, sugar and milk are brought to a boil then several tempered egg yolks and vanilla are added then simmered until yellow and thick. It is usually served warm over cold desserts. After dessert there was a perpetual cheese board, then it was back to one's same seat for the remainder of the evening until precisely 11:00 for coffee and Cointreau or Drambuie.

One had to create a dinner at home as sumptuous as possible, since restaurants were not only awful in the provinces but mingling with the masses strictly infra dig. The higher the station of the guests the finer the meal had to be. Jaffe and Haskell had, however, endured the graduate students' polite chatter bloody long enough and felt no need to talk to anyone but each other, also ignoring their dutiful wives. We became accustomed to such pecking order rudeness in the Groves of Academe but as a consequence I have studiously avoided any of the aboves' art historical pronouncements on Rubens or patronage. Seeking psychological revenge I thought how Roger Fry would have been full of curiosity about young people unlike these tradesmen, these arrivistes, these parvenus.

Richard introduced us to Malcolm Cormack, the director of the Fitzwilliam Museum, whom we invited to dinner in the now slightly pruned Pre-Raphaelite garden. A grammar school boy (a distinct type, decidedly not public school and very much on the ascent) Malcolm was handsome and enchanting but on the very night of the *diner sur l'herbe* his wife was taken ill, rather a common occurrence at that time! Rather than cancel when we heard, which would have been far less embarrassing, we soldiered on as Malcolm arrived with a bottle of claret, which he expected to share with several others. Regretted it would be just us three, his fallen face, oh dear, we rushed through the Navarin Printanier and henceforth I always asked three or four couples for dinner just in case another wife or two fell ill. Minimum four guests, maximum ten became my rule for sit-down dinners and for more guests a buffet was offered. Nothing is worse than a command performance and Malcolm never warmed to us again, understandably. Faux Pas!

Speaking of command performances, I subjected E.M. Forster to one when I requested a meeting to discuss Bloomsbury. He was in his 90s, crippled by a broken hip, his pale blue eyes clouded over with glaucoma, but still full of vitality as he ordered tea and shortbread for the stranger in his digs at King's. His politeness and reticence ("Liked Fry. Good fellow.") at this advanced age were still pronounced and he cared not to chat about *Howard's End* but chuckled about Bloomsbury painting ("looked like I was dropped from the clouds onto a pillow" of his portrait) and really rather how awful it all was. Or so he thought. Did I agree? Actually did I really think there was anything called the Bloomsbury Group? He surely didn't. Well maybe he was wrong. On his walls were Picasso pink period posters of circus boys in the dark shadows of the room. How did so many Englishmen get so shy? The lack of light? Damp weather? Being an island? After this embarrassing intrusion I cancelled meetings with Duncan Grant and Leonard Woolf which of course I now regret.

UP NORTH

"To leave the North was an act of betrayal as well as folly. In the South they rode to hounds and went to Ascot; in the North we kept pigeons and raced greyhounds. When we had our tea, people in London sat down to their dinner dressed up as if they were off to a Masonic hot-pot supper."

Beryl Bainbridge, *Forever England.*

Lee was offered a lectureship in history at the brand new University of Lancaster so we moved north the year after Churchill's funeral and stayed until the Vietnam War ended, and a bit beyond. North Lancashire, on the border of Cumbria, then called Westmorland and Cumberland, was located around the 55th parallel, about the same latitude as Leningrad, but sported a far milder climate due to the Gulf Stream. It also had the highest density rainfall, a gloomy 80 to 100 inches a year, in the British Isles, the epicenter being the village of Garstang, a mile or two down the road from our house. In this Land of the Red Rose, the home of the ancient house of the Plantagenet Kings, we saw plenty of faded plastic reminders of the 15th century conflict between Edward IV and the White Rose's Henry VI of York on restaurant tables and in boarding room windows.

This was a remote, hilly region of Britain, with lush and lovely dales between high fells, heather moors and the Pennine Mountains, "the backbone of England" dividing East and West from the Peak District to the Cheviot Hills on the Scots border. Much of the Northwest possessed a treeless lunar landscape not without its portentous rain drenched charms, but Lancaster was just an old decayed county town struggling to get by. The biggest industry was the

Royal Lancaster Hospital before the University set up shop. Remarking that they should have called it the Royal Lancaster University, we spent our first night at the Royal Kings Arms Hotel, a derelict 19th century railroad hotel, where one solitary lightbulb hung from the cracked plaster ceiling. It had obviously seen better days. All of the town had seen better days, centuries ago before the Lune River silted over and commerce ground to a halt. In 1823 a penny newspapers noted that Lancaster, with 40,000 souls, was in decay and century and a half later nothing much had changed. Today the population is still about the same.

Lancaster was a Plate Glass university, established under the Labour government along with Sussex, York, Warwick, Essex, to distinguish it from the Red Bricks such as Manchester and Reading. It opened in 1964 at a plot of land, Bailrigg, (in old Norse *bail* is the forest limit and *rigg* the boundary, of the ancient and now non-existent Forest of Bowland) two miles south of the town, all mud roads and construction in the black rain and howling winds. It was still that way when we arrived. These few acres of civilization were to be our refuge in this land with 25% of the population on the Dole, poor souls living on tea and toast amidst crumbling linen and cotton mills, with outdoor loos and certainly no central heating in the row houses built by Baron Ashton. In 1907 the cotton king also built a giant mausoleum in memory of his wife Jessy which still graced the highest promontory of the town. A green life-sized statue of Queen Victoria also peered down on her subjects from nearby Dalton Square.

Rebecca Fraser's *The Story of Britain*, a long sweep over the timeline from B.C. to the present, referred to the period 1964-1979, almost exactly corresponding to our sojourn, as the time when England was The Sick Man of Europe. Nowhere more so than in the North. The University was consequently seething with anti-Establishment feeling and the younger lecturers passionately supported workers' rights amidst wage freezes, countless strikes and oil crises, and as always "rampant" inflation. It got so bad the government had to subsidize butter as it had always subsidized the permanently go-slow British Rail. The

Labour Party was as suspect and despised as the Tories and Harold Wilson was mocked and ridiculed for supporting America in Vietnam and trying to break the backs of the unions.

I wrote in my journals that the North was "the backyard of the world, immortalized as the Seat of Hell in many a Dickens novel, where the trees are blackly silhouetted against a low sky, rather like living under a tea cosey." Charles Dickens had in fact visited Lancaster several times to gain inspiration for his novels. One hundred years later the mills and factories might have gone silent but nothing replaced them leaving a desolate emptiness, massive unemployment and great poverty. Roger Fry thought it resembled Dante's Inferno, and Defoe had found it a place of "inhospitable terror" but it was less the landscape than the poverty of the people in a land that had been invaded since the Stone Age by everyone from Romans to Danes and Norwegians to Normans that was so profound. The North of England seemed to be recovering from the Second World War but in fact it was still recuperating from the Industrial Revolution.

One of our dwellings, two adjacent row houses knocked together at 10 St. Mary's Parade, faced Lancaster Priory Church and Lancaster Castle, the site of the Pendle Witch Trials of 1612. Visitors flocked to the Hanging Town's dungeon where the accused endured total darkness before they were strung up or burned in what had previously been the site of a Roman garrison. Much of Northern England had relics that predated the Romans, the stone circle of Castlerigg that John Keats called "a dismal cirque of Druid stones upon a forlorn moor" or Heysham's dramatic Viking rock hewn graves leading down to the sea from St. Peter's Church. A few miles away, near Carlisle was the western most part of Hadrian's Wall and mile after mile or Roman roads, straight as arrows, joining east and west. Lancaster had sacrificed its original Roman ruins to London and only dusty, chipped plaster copies remained in the museum in town.

As Lee was lecturing about poor relief four hundred years ago, I experienced its need daily teaching English at Our Lady's Roman Catholic High School, a comprehensive school for 10-13 year olds, mostly of Irish descent. I later taught Western culture at Harris College in Preston to the same lads a few years older, on day—release programs from British Leyland, always marveling at their accurate assessments of cultural artifacts such as *Guernica*: "That's right daft M'am!" Preston! Where Catholics were exiled in the 17th century, one of those "insensate industrial towns" the very birthplace of radicalism and trade unionism where Richard Arkwright's Water Frame that brought the cotton mills up North, was invented. In 1842 the millworkers demonstrated against the horrid conditions they endured fourteen hours a day, which prompted Karl Marx to come from his home in Manchester thirty miles away.

I also lectured in Liverpool, still festooned with bombed out ruins from the War, at the Open University another Labour effort in higher education where students studied at home then came for a weekly evening seminar, always looking tired after a day's work. And in much maligned and perfectly named Blackpool where 14-year old Alfred Cooke, son of a pipefitter, won a scholarship in a comprehensive school and escaped to Jesus College, Cambridge changing his name to Alistair. To historians the Oxford don A.J.P. Taylor's Lancashire origins were always discussed however much they sneered at his popularization of the sacred historical past on the bloody boob tube and more so by his pretense of being a poor cheeky Lancashireman when in fact he hailed from the haute bourgeoisie and had gone to Oriel.

THE BLITZ AND THE BEATLES

Memories of World War II, rationing and the Blitz, were still very vivid, everyone having lived through the hard times and longing to share their experiences. We Americans might have burst red dots to make white margarine yellow but the English stored eggs in the earth, (you were only allowed one a week, if that) preserving them in isinglass or nail polish, and bribed farmers for potatoes with grandfather's pearl tie pin. Rationing started in 1939 and did not end until 1954 and the stoic Brits endured it for fifteen long years, the mock sausage, mock lobster and mock everything made from porridge pretending to be animal protein. (Mock turtle, a stuffed sheep's head, was still a Lancashire staple). The camaraderie in the Tube during the bombings, so well captured in the drawings of Henry Moore, and how the Home Army outsmarted Hitler were also favorite subjects of reverie. The head of Lancaster's History Department, Austin Woolrych, lost an eye at El Alamein and my friend Jane Henriquez Egan's father was Patton's chief aide. Between the legacy of the Industrial Revolution and the Blitz no wonder the country had such an abysmal culinary reputation.

In the Spring 2006 issue of *This England* Miss Edna Branthwaite recalls foraging for wild food, plants, seeds, leaves and fruit in Cumberland as a child during the long years of rationing. "For herb pudding the children collected nettle leaves, hawthorn leaves, sour docking, and Easter 'mangiants'. These, along with a small stick of rhubarb, spring cabbage, a leek and an onion were finely chopped, covered in cold water to which three dessertspoons of pearl barley were added and cooked slowly in the oven. When the barley was cooked a tablespoon of havermeal (oatmeal) and 2 eggs were added and back into the oven to be further cooked then served at every Easter Sunday lunch to cleanse the blood". The children also harvested bilberries (bleaberries), cranberries and Rose hips, which were rounded up from 1943 by County Herb Committees to distribute throughout the Isle as a substitute for the Vitamin C of citrus fruits, which were almost impossible to obtain.

As the world was idolizing the Beatles, in the same year as Woodstock, we were dancing to the live music of Bill Haley's *Rock Around the Clock* in Morecambe's old Art Deco Midland Hotel where the aging bandleader singer cranked out music while we drank warm bitters. My old idol from Birdland days Maynard Ferguson also entertained us in the same hotel and "time warp" is not doing the experience justice. It was a surrealistic juxtaposition of time and space, living in the back end of the Western world where the Beatles were born and whence they fled.

One of my colleagues at Harris, John Lane, had attended Liverpool Art School at the same time as John and Paul. He often entertained us with stories such as Lennon's being a disturbed vandal, an orphan living with an old aunt and smashing idols (literally) in religious shops. He also recalled seeing him perform on the lunch room table with McCartney and like everyone else in Lancashire claimed he had discovered the Beatles before Brian Epstein. We visited the Cavern Club on Mathew Street right before it was demolished and indeed it was a cave, a dark Troglodyte environment reminiscent of the mines where workers were imprisoned as they fueled the gaping maw of the factories. Perhaps you can only truly understand the nostalgic and melancholy songs of the Beatles if you know the working men's clubs that proliferated in the North, those smoky, beery halls with live vaudeville, tales of opportunities missed and bad breaks.

The Beatles were mad and sad at the inequities of English culture, a spirit Lennon never lost; the vegetarian hippy lifestyle of McCartney and the guru seeking of Harrison were folk art variations of the outsider. The vaudevillian, wry comical and poignant tradition of Lancashire could be seen in local talent such as Gracie Fields, Stan Laurel, John Mahoney and *Jaws'* Quint, Robert Shaw.

Lest you thought there would be no sustenance . . .

VITTLES AND CLASS

The British Empire and its legacy existed in the souls and on the tables of 55 million people in the 1960s and 70s and status was still defined not by what you wore or had in the bank but by your birth and accent. This gave many a sinecure for life and we had several friends of the right class who lived on lifelong overdrafts from Barclay's Bank in large, draughty historic houses. In the North cooking and social class were inseparable, reflecting the heritage of urban industrial life and a millennium of farming hard land and herding sheep in a bad climate. Simple, hearty unadorned fare for working men in town or country, it was as much cucina povera as the pasta asciutta so despised by Marinetti. Farmers and factory workers ate starchy, fatty and sugary foods out of habit and cultural solidarity. They'd be damned if they would give up their grease bread! Or Players. Or bitters.

Lancaster Market, built in the last years of Victoria's reign, of wood from what remained of the Forest of Bowland, depleted by Fleetwood's and Barrow-in-Furness' ship building industry, was located in a damp, dark structure in the center of town on Penny Street. It burned down in the 1980s and its replacement is considered ugly, cold and empty and one suspects that economic prospects are no brighter today than they were when I shopped daily in the market. Fisherman's Friends by the way are still made in Fleetwood, those eucalyptus and menthol lozenges found at every drugstore in the United States for a hundred years and which soothed the throats of sailors and fishermen of this busy port on the Fylde, the site of a lost Roman port.

On Saturdays in the marketplace clog dancing troops held competitions from time to time. A percussion dance, its origins were in

40

the Satanic mills where men and woman wore wooden soled shoes to keep their feet dry and whose clattering sound mimicked the weaving machines. It is like Morris dancing but performed sonorously with cleats on black boots worn by miners, millworkers, and the fish bobbers who unloaded boats. I wore wooden soled shoes (sans cleats) all the time in my years in Lancashire. It made as much sense as eating sheep and burning coal.

The classic class distinctions, aristocracy-gentry-merchants-farmers-servants-laborers existed in our lives as landed gentry, the middle class, i.e., professors, doctors and whatnot, the working class and the rarely spotted aristocracy. Princess Alexandra was the Chancellor of the University of Lancaster and she paid an annual visit that brought out the absolute worst in everyone, including liberals and anarchists, all jockeying for position to bow and grovel. When the Queen paid a visit in 1971 en route to Scotland, the town worthies only painted that part of the station she would actually see from her window knowing she would not likely get off the train and head over Skerton Bridge to Morecambe.

Royalty was of little or no interest to the lads and lasses in my classrooms. Many a time when I brought up the Queen *et.cie* they would guffaw or snicker and never once in all those years did I ever find a royalist or monarchist or apologist for the Crown. (We "intellectuals" lauded Tony Benn for renouncing his peerage). With typical British apathy the working class seemed to acquiesce in the class structure, it being imponderable that life should be otherwise. When I called royalty an insult to every workingman in my most radical days in the War of Words, it elicited no response from the navvies, just utter indifference.

It was a relatively quiet time for the Windsors compared with the madness of tabloid Britain today. I often wonder how it has all gotten so out of hand but I think I know: more leisure time and no liberal, humanizing education and of course the god-awful demographic explosion. The tabloids never appeared on our table though after—dinner conversation would inevitably turn to the "T and A" press and what a cad Beaverbrook was and an ocean of opinions swirled in a scenario where you always preached to the choir. Unlike Princeton there was no dissent because everyone agreed the Tories were ghastly, the workers were oppressed, America was a capitalist conspiracy and the Vietnam War as much genocide as the Holocaust.

We planned our weekend excursions away from Lancaster with great resolve. If we weren't scrambling up the steep gradients of Scafell, England's highest mountain, Great Gable or Helvellyn's fearsome Striding Edge, or rambling in heather, bracken and gorse we prowled around Ewan Kerr's bookshop in Kendal. Here I found a first edition, complete with Brantwood bookplates and owlish handwritten notes, of Ruskin's *Tintoretto* later stolen in Chicago. Or we went to Manchester to Terrence Conran's houseware store, Habitat, making a whole day of it, perusing cooking equipment, cast iron crepe pans, (we had three sizes), great enameled casseroles, French soufflé dishes, white and fluted, tin apparatus like the rickety little Mouli mill for grinding parsley and garlic, my essential kitchen companion. Afterwards we would hit one of the old Manchester pubs before heading forty miles up the M6 to get ready for a dinner party. So much of life was about eating and drinking, at least in Academic Leisure Land and as a friend Nick Oulton opined, "Life is just one beverage after another, isn't it?"

BUTTIES AND BARMS

In the winter the sun set at 3 P.M. in the North and I discovered a population that revered darkness, in foods like parkin or hot pot, or in art. During lectures about the Fauves at Harris the lads complained how the brightness and all those colors hurt their eyes and at Our Lady's pupils got headaches if the sun was out too long. After a few weeks in a damp house without central heating, hot tea and sugary biscuits were craved constantly. I have never figured out the physiology of all this but it has eluded writers like Waverly Root who considered this love of highly seasoned and sugared food somehow an aberration. He probably never lived in England. Elizabeth David also snootily commented on this penchant but then again she would never have known the navvies only the trout and pheasant loving upper classes.

Every day I shopped for food in Lancaster Market or in the little shops on the winding medieval back streets because we had no fridge but also because I had not lost any of my passion for marketing. My first stop was usually Postlethwaite's Bakery which sports another Old Norse name, the ubiquitous *thwaite* meaning a clearing in the forest, perhaps the dwelling of a *postle*, a notary. It offered a wooly, crumbly whole grain loaf which I plopped in a string bag, nattering with the locals about the beastly weather and beastly economy. Most baked goods at Postlethwaite's and the other local bakeries had the place names of Lancashire and Lakeland towns, Eccles Cakes, Chorley Cakes, Goosnargh Cakes, Oldham Parkin, Ambleside Gingerbread, Grasmere Gingerbread, Preston Gingerbread, Honister Cheesecake, Coniston Cheesecake, Lonsdale Scones, Cumberland Nickies, Lakeland Tatie Scones, Windermere Spice Biscuits, Bury Simnel Cakes,

Manchester Pudding, Lancashire Bun Loaf, to name a few. Parkin, a dark, heavy gingerbread, is quintessentially Northern fare, both Red and White Rose sides of the country, gritty, earthy, no frills. A hearty slab could sustain you for a whole day.

Yorkshire was a few minutes away just over the Pennines so we made regular forays across the border to visit Vanbrugh's Castle Howard with Hawksmoor's Temple of the Four Winds and Capability Brown's landscaping, or the romantic ruins of ancient abbeys such as Fountains or Rielvaux (in the years before Harold Wilson, a local lad from Huddersfield, comically became Lord of the same name). We took tea at the Bowes Museum in Barnard Castle which had a spectacular collection of oil paintings from Boucher to Tiepolo and decorative arts from that time in European civilization when the rich were even richer, and intent on squeezing the farmers off the land with the system of enclosures.

Yorkshire claims parkin as its local contribution to heritage cuisine and it is always served on Guy Fawke's Night, November 5th, but it was also omnipresent in Lancashire. Most Lancashire parkin contains finely ground oatmeal, treacle (molasses), Lyle's golden syrup, lard, butter, eggs, Demerara sugar, and a goodly amount of ground ginger. The result is something between bread and cake in consistency, and not too sweet. Grasmere Gingerbread is more fancy, made with flour, candied peel, ginger and brown sugar and no treacle and sponge parkin is somewhere in between the two using half oatmeal and half flour. Preston had its own fine version as well.

Cakes, breads, teacakes, cobblers, puddings, custards, creams, junkets, jellies, compotes, fools, syllabubs, pies, tarts, pasties, biscuits and wigs abounded in the local cuisine all variations of sugar, flour, fat and sometimes eggs. They had to be life-sustaining because I saw more old men in the North than anywhere else in the world, tall, thin 80 and 90 year olds taking the train from Giggleswick to Leeds or Lancaster to Giggleswick in their tweed caps and long overcoats. Their wives were always chunkier, but they lived long lives, hale and hearty with great smoky, throaty laughs. This was high Alf Wight country, the local vet who wrote under the nom de guerre James Herriot.

Most of the floury fare had very similar ingredients imported from the West Indies for centuries in exchange for wool. Dried fruits like figs, prunes, currants, sultanas, almonds, and spices such as cinnamon, nutmeg, cloves, ginger, caraway or allspice and of course Barbados sugar and rum were omnipresent in cooking in both sweet and savoury dishes. Eccles Cakes were banned by the Puritans, sinful flaky pastry filled with dried fruit and spices gathered up like a beggar's purse then turned over and slashed three times to let steam escape. The larger Chorley Cake or Banbury Cake was basically the same, candied peel, currants and allspice wrapped up in flaky pastry. I especially liked the strange cross between bread and cake called Goosnargh Cakes named for the town a few miles north of Preston where Chingle Hall is said to be the most haunted house in England, buttery biscuits with a good sprinkling of caraway seeds. Wonderful Bakewell tarts named for a town a little farther south in Derbyshire, made with ground almonds and jam in a shortcrust pastry.

Lamplugh pudding was not a pastry or a bread but a sort of porridge named for a coastal port town near Workington on the West Coast. A Cumbrian hill farmer's dish created to warm up the eater after a bitterly cold day of lambing, it consists of brown ale mulled with cloves, allspice and cinnamon, lemon juice and rind, sugar, to which rolled oats and crushed biscuits are added. It was traditionally served at Christmas or on Boxing Day, that national holiday so celebrated by anti-clerical Academia and the only day of the year it was acceptable to pop by a friend's house unannounced.

Colin Spencer notes that the poor in the cities "had never seen a wheatfield or realized that it had any connection with bread" but bakeries and teashops flourished in the North with their barmcakes and floury baps. Barm, the ancient word for the froth after yeast is proofed, became a barmcake or roll if it was made with whole wheat flour and a bap if white flour. Baps and not barms were used for bacon butties, the regional sandwich, of a slice of Danish bacon, not streaky but lean with a thin rind of snow white fat. It always struck me as odd that in the land of 300 strong pig farms bacon was imported, but that is a matter of economic history.

Other sandwiches, called British Railways Sandwiches because they were served in local stations, were made from large white loaves sliced very thin, with crumbled Lancashire cheese and thinly sliced onion, or Heinz beans on toast, or chips (French fries) on toast, or ham and crisps, those salty potato chips put right inside the sandwich, or sliced hard boiled egg, cress and tomato on a long roll with salad cream, a vinegary sort of mayonnaise. All were very good and tasted best in cold damp waiting rooms with plenty of hot sugary tea. Who can forget the Goon Show's *Collapse of the British Railway Sandwich System* and the vagaries that befell the cress and mustard sandwich in the 1954 farce with Peter Sellers? It was prescient since sandwiches in stations were soon to disappear.

VEGGIES AND FRUITS

Fruits and vegetables were abundant in Lancaster Market and as Jane Grigson states time and again in *English Food* the inhabitants of the green scepter'd isle were once great vegetable eaters before the depredations of the Industrial Revolution. The effect of a century of mass production, imported food, and the decline of locally produced foods was still very much in evidence when I lived in the Sick Man of Europe, with food consumption for the working class as a low point. The Rare Breeds Survival Trust was however just founded and the era of canned mushy peas was achangin'. In 1967 the Agricultural Act was passed and a wary eye was cast on pesticides and factory farming heralding the beginning of the organic health food movement.

Greengrocers in Lancaster Market offered a great variety of vegetables, expensive little Dutch tomatoes, several varieties of local mushrooms, snow white cauliflower, foot-long green marrows, and sprouts, so many kinds, watercress, and plain cress, curly little shoots still in their earthy gardens, and perpetual brussel sprouts. There were green courgettes (zucchini), Spring onions (scallions), aubergines (eggplants) which were transformed into garlicky baba ganoush or Pantry Caviar, cucumbers of all sizes, asparagus in the summer and root vegetables, neeps (turnips) and potatoes and carrots and parsnips which were always available year round as was The Leek.

The noble leek which I had first failed to clean properly in that early Vichyssoise now appeared on our dinner table a la Greque, or in a shortcrust pastry tart with Lancashire or white Stilton cheese. It was at its glory paired with a chicken, two ingredients enough to make an entire flavorful dish, Cock A Leekie soup, and if a touch of curry powder, some yogurt and a prune or two were added it became Mulligatawny soup. There was no evidence in Lancaster Market of sea kale or samphire which besides the leek are supposedly the only uniquely indigenous English vegetables. Nettles and edible dandelions were, however, everywhere.

I became a virtuoso of brussel sprouts and cooked them variously, as soup, which like all the watery breed consisted of sautéed onion, chicken stock, salt and pepper, then enhanced by cream or milk. They were sautéed in bacon fat, with shallots and hazelnuts or sometimes combined with brown lentils, a hint of curry powder and a dollop of sour cream. If the tomatoes were hard they emerged *a la Provencal* sprinkled with Parmesan, breadcrumbs, parsley, a little garlic and what remained of that olive oil we lugged back from Nimes, then baked in the Aga. Stuffing also reigned supreme in marrows a true Lancashire specialty containing leftover lamb, onions and rice or root vegetables or anything you had in the larder. Like white bread it had no taste whatsoever and served as a perfect foil for whatever was added. Courgettes were plentiful and I baked them with tomatoes and studiously avoided making ratatouille, which tasted as bitter as Gauloises.

Colcannon (or Bubble and Squeak if fried), cabbage shredded and mixed with mashed potatoes and onions was rarely, if ever, undertaken, much too plebian to serve to guests and much too much work for 6:00 meals. When a cabbage appeared it was fermented as sauerkraut which was bought prepared, refreshed in water, sautéed with a little bacon, onion, an Oxo cube and caraway seeds and cooked for a long time in the oven, the basis for my party piece, Choucroute Garni. Cauliflower was usually served Polonaise style with fried breadcrumbs, or prettily pureed with a touch of yellow turmeric and butter or as a proper souffle with a hint of cheese. In the fine restaurants in the North great big bowls of vegetables with butter and salt and pepper appeared at tables along with the main course and they were plain and superb.

Fruits were mainly berries and damson plums, some seasonal apples and of course rhubarb. One is surprised given the lack of sun that they existed at all and that they contained any sugar. Ask why the English working class eats so much sugar, starch and fat and the answer is right there, they burn as cheap fuel in the body. There were gooseberries, currants, wimberries, bilberries, cranberries, rowanberries, crabapples, blackberries (those luscious brambles from our Cambridge days), quince and medlars, the name of a new gastro pub in Cockermouth and deep purple, sour, beautiful damson plums, called witherslacks, grown just south of Lake Windermere in the Lyth Valley.

One of the few fruits that can grow in an inhospitable climate these little purple plums made superb jam, with natural pectin, a fine balance of sweet and sour and a distinct plumby taste. A syllabub of the jam, with gin, cream and egg whites always served with Grasmere Gingerbread or Windermere Spiced Biscuits and a local specialty was Damson Gin made from the juice of the fruit, gin and sugar to taste. Quite a beverage! Today you can buy it from Cowmire Hall in Kendal.

FOR THE LOVE OF
BLACK PUDDING

Lancashire was the home not only of the bacon butty but of The Black Pudding a sausage of congealed pig's blood, oatmeal and plenty of pepper, served steaming in the corner shop and like fish n'chips eaten with malt vinegar. It never passed these lips. The author of *The Cumbrian Trilogy*, novelist and man of letters Lord Melvyn Bragg was born in Wigton, Cumbria and recently emailed me recalling the black puddings of his youth from Middleham's in Wigton and the Cumberland sausage from Fox's in the same town, and fresh eggs from the Farmers' Market.

In the first book of his trilogy, the history of 20th century Northern English life, *The Hired Man,* he lists the ingredients of A Great Feast for Hundreds served in 1919 in a Cumberland village to celebrate the end of the War: "ninety pounds of beef, ready cut, six boiled hams, over a hundredweight of potatoes, two roasted legs of ham, two of pork, a stone of green peas, two dozen cauliflowers, two dozen cabbage and a stone of split peas, eight hundred teacakes, as well as bread and cakes and biscuits, dozens of jars of home-made jam, pints of cream and preserves, twelve plum puddings, twelve rice puddings, rum sauce for the plum puddings, Crossbridge Pudding (buns steeped until soft in hot ale and served with seasonings and spirits to taste), and twelve herb puddings, including rhubarb, nettles, blackcurrant leaves, cabbage, cauliflower, leeks, sour dockings, barley, Easter mangiants—twenty-one different ingredients topped by whisked eggs." Just like Edna Branthwaite's!

Starch, grease and offal appears in the memories of Lancashire lad (well not really a lad, he went to Oxford) George Orwell who gave rather a bad name to his home county with a description of the working class fondness for dirty tripe served in a loathsome a shop in Wigan. While there was still plenty of tripe in Wigan and Lancaster I could never even look at it no less eat it, nor brains, nor pigs' heads, nor the heads of lambs, nor udders, testicles, trotters or cow heels, not even sweetbreads or tongue.

Besides *Road to Wigan Pier* Orwell also wrote a defense of English cooking in the 1950s (had he read Elizabeth David?) in which he disputed the claim that it is merely French cooking. He reminded the reader that English cooking was kippers, Yorkshire puddings, Devonshire cream, muffins and crumpets and puddings, and biscuits and potato cakes and dried fish for the poor. All in all his picture of Wigan was far more sympathetic than Paul Theroux' fifty years later when the city was demoralized by the Dole, high unemployment, post industrial slump and an eerie silence. He called it one of the "horror cities" of the North but I found it had a homely charm with sweet people abounding and a great esprit de corps that solitary rail travelers who dash through towns can never experience.

The food of the North lured the author of *A Clockwork Orange*, one of the films we then revered, Anthony Burgess, back to his roots. In his autobiographical essays collected in *One Man's Chorus*, he waxed nostalgic about the earthy grimness of the food which perfectly reflected the culture and the landscape: chip butties, hotpot with scrag's neck of lamb (we knew ye well), meat and potato pie, barm cake, of course tripe, of course black pudding, especially Lancashire black pudding,

Eccles cakes, Bakewell tarts, jam puffs, and baked custards in crusty pastry and what he called the king of Northern dishes, Lancashire Hotpot which he remembered was served with pickled red cabbage and I recall served with beets.

SPRECKLED FRY

We lived a couple of miles from the Irish Sea and Morecambe Bay and were surrounded by lakes and rivers and streams and deep black tarns so fish were abundant. Salting and smoking, the oldest ways to preserve food, and local cures abounded for pork and fish. The working poor ate salted, smoked sea fish, while the gentry, the squirearchy as we wryly called them, and we middle classes consumed freshwater fish. From the lakes and the rivers that flow down to the sea, from the Pennines and Cheviots, were char, a small relative of the salmon and scarce, rainbow or brown trout and large salmon. In the 18th and 19th centuries Englishmen traveled all the way up to Lake Windermere to eat the famous char served for breakfast in little white porcelain char pots in which they were baked with butter.

The taste and qualities of sea fish such as hake, cod, halibut and plaice were utterly transformed by a batter blanket encasing the delicate flesh which was deep-fried in tasty suet. Voila fish and chips. We boycotted this national dish since the ink from the newspaper cones seemed toxic and although plastic cones would replace the *Sun* or the *Mirror* the smell of malt vinegar and roasted newspaper lingered in the soul forever. Fish and chips is often said to be classless but very few of our friends would be seen dead in the smoke and grease filled corner chippy.

John and Di King were the far other side of the middle class academic. John, an anarcho syndicalist, earned a scholarship in grammar school to Jesus College like Alistair Cooke, but unlike him never wished to renounce or forget his working class roots. He embraced them, he flouted them. We were invited to his home for supper at six and Di, rotund and nearly toothless, greeted us with a "coooooome on in". The fat in the simmering chip pot was odiferous to say the least and later that week caught fire and actually burned down the kitchen. The brussel sprouts had obviously been boiling for an hour or two, then the battered fish and some quartered potatoes were dropped into the sizzling suet and a bit o' lard. There was no corkscrew for the wine we brought so Di simply cracked off its neck as 5 year old Cheryl walked by and called her a silly bitch. They were certainly not aping upper class mores as so many others did with their pewter chargers and antique brass candlesticks and clarets breathing on polished Georgian sideboards.

Cockles and mussels were plentiful and cheap as was mackerel and dried herring, called kippers, hopefully smoked over oak but often just dyed orange. Herring flourished in the North Sea since the 11th century and was as much a part of English history, a form of currency, as cod or sheep. For parties, I served mounds of mussels as we sat on Moroccan pillows listening to Mahavishnu or the mellifluous voice of the poet David Craig defend Communism, workers' rights, the Celtic love of the land as we ate garlicky, peppery red tomato sauce enhancing the salty mussels. It was a time of enormous political activism at the University. Lee was a founding member of ASTMS, a union formed to represent the rights of junior non-tenured lecturers. They occupied the administration building with a hundred students for several days, which resulted in a small raise for the university janitors, but alas no guarantees for the lecturers.

Unfortunately the Vice Chancellor Charles Carter blamed everything on the Communists and David Craig and the Craig Affair became the Lancaster Affair, which escalated more and more until he was fired, accused of favoring politically correct answers on his English exams, penalizing those who did not tow the party line. There were more huge demonstrations with supporters from universities all over the British Isles and countless building occupations, which threatened to shut down the university. Craig was eventually rehired but is probably still sneering at Professor Bill Murray and the English Department.

Amongst all this tumult I made gooseberry sauce for mackerel, the tart yellow berries sprinkled with a bit of sugar, cooked in butter, breadcrumbs, and cayenne and served with the grilled fish. You could also add cooked gooseberries to a béchamel sauce, mash it a bit and pour it over the fish but this was a bit rich for mackerel. If you didn't have gooseberries, rhubarb would do just fine. Trout was served for dinner once a week, always whole, stuffed with parsley, celery and sautéed onions (never ever garlic which does not belong with fish, any fish, any time) and baked in buttered parchment paper. Oysters were plentiful as well and were common in Morecambe restaurants, a treat we saved for visiting Frenchmen or Germans. They sometimes appeared if requested in Lancashire Hotpot.

Finnan haddie or haddock cold smoked in the style of Findon near Aberdeen was steeped in hot water, flaked, added to boiled rice, hard boiled eggs, melted butter and parsley for a British Heritage dish. Kedgeree, a name evoking the colonial past, was always dry as a bone so I served it with a curry cream sauce for Sunday brunch when we invited all the bachelors in the department over. They would marry soon enough but at the time were a perfect and appreciative single male audience, tall, aloof Tony Tuck, impossibly sweet David Holloway, irreverent sourball Gordon Phillips, Falstaffian Marcus Merriman from Baltimore, seriously witty Ivor Crew, a salon of sorts where I was a veritable Georges Sand though I am sure the bachelors came for the Kedgeree or Salmon Pie. The latter was a variation of Russian coulibiaca, containing economically thinly sliced fresh salmon, cooked rice, diced onions, mushrooms, parsley, all placed in alternate layers and baked in prepared puff pastry. Melted butter was poured into slits on the top right before serving.

MORECAMBE

Shrimp was synonymous the country over with the desolate little sister of Blackpool adjacent to Lancaster—the holiday town of Morecambe—with its tiny, brown *Crangon crangon,* which were already scarce thirty or forty years ago. Paul Theroux noted that it was odd indeed for a seaside resort to be built in the rainiest place in Britain and moreover on a muddy bay, but like Wigan, Morecambe possessed a certain non-bourgeois charm, a notion very appealing at the time.

Shrimp had been potted and preserved in there since 1799 when nets first scooped them up and loaded the bounty onto carts; today tractors are used, still a dicey business due to the quicksand and tides that can ambush you from all angles. Once the tractors bring in the shrimps they are boiled in seawater, peeled and potted with melted butter. My eco minded friend Dick Frost recently wrote that they are probably fluorescent by now (a reference to Windscale the nuclear power plant, a hideous and frightening sight looming in the bucolic North). Potted Shrimp is a British Heritage dish in which you boil shrimp, add butter, and spices like mace, nutmeg and cayenne, place in ramekins and cover with a thin layer of clarified butter. It will keep for weeks and the same method can be used for any potted fish. Shrimp, however, are particularly nice.

Walking the nine-mile stretch across Morecambe Bay when the tide receded was the staple subject of 19th century engravings, an adventure to rank with seeing the Pyramids, and an attraction for generations of

British visitors including the Duke of Edinburgh. From time to time we trekked the four long wet hours across the treacherous Bay fearing the return of the fastest tides in the British Isles, guided by an expert who knew just where the quicksand was, but who could not avoid the chest high streams we had to wade through or the millions of coiled worms on the ocean floor. One's expensive Swiss hiking boots were ruined after one of these ventures.

Perhaps only the English would submit to the profound discomfort of an exhausting walk in the cold with wet clothing and sopping boots which never dried even after a couple of hours in a damp pub in our destination, Grange-Over-Sands. Like the sinister and foggy treks on the fells, fear and suffering, then mystic relief when it was over afforded a sort of reward. Physical stoicism or indifference to material comfort is a trait shared by all classes in Britannia. In our unheated stone dwellings over the years visiting guests from America or the Continent would return home with pneumonia and I had for years a crippling case of chilblains from sodden toes placed too close to coal fires. Bill Bryson accurately comments on the "curious attitude of the British to pleasure" but we knew it was a legacy of Puritanism and the absolute absence of a pleasurable climate but I found it bracing after awhile and it took some years to adjust to the comfort mania and materialism of America.

Along the boardwalk in Morecambe were rows of B & Bs and old boarding houses that offered damp beds with copper warming pans filled with coals, as well as 'full English' breakfasts of fried brown—shelled eggs, a slab of grease bread, a singular experience, streaky bacon, black pudding if requested, a tomato and a wee mushroom. This was the ubiquitous breakfast demanded in every Northern county and if you were not a calorie-burning farmer chasing sheep you felt like the proverbial lead balloon until late in the day. Such a far cry was it from the silvered buffet breakfasts of shirred eggs and caviar in the country homes of Olde England.

FAIR FOWLS

Speaking of which, the game hall in Lancaster Market displayed pheasants, partridge, grouse, woodcock, pigeons, all still befeathered and colorfully strung up though they were too daunting to purchase since I could not pluck a bird with the sang froid of my French friends. We tried to import shotguns from Wisconsin to join in the Non-U sport of bird shooting on the moors but alas that was impossible since the Home Office reserved that pleasure for the gentry and gun licenses were impossible to obtain. Besides much of the best grouse shooting moorland was on the Queen's estate, she being The Duke of Lancaster of The Duchy of Lancaster, where bailiffs were ever ready with shotgun in hand to ward you off if the gargantuan snorting black bulls did not scare you off first. (We had bolted over a fence or two in our walking life).

Ergo, a *Gosford Park* shootout was a no-go as was the fancy brunch afterwards in Robert Altman's odd take on the English at play. Academics, members of the "gown", just tolerated by the professional "town" worthies, doctors and solicitors and retired civil servants, if they wanted the gentry experience, had to be content with horseback riding on the treacherous, hedged motor roads, and were decidedly not invited to ride to the hunt (in the animal-loving North a live fox was replaced by a wooden one). Like shooting grouse on the moors, chasing foxes on horseback was consigned to the Bludleigh Courts of Wodehouse's imagination as he wrote in exile on Long Island. I took to the horse with trepidation as I jumped over cavalleti and attempted dressage, always glad when the ordeal on the back of huge chestnut mares was over.

We ate fine fowl whenever possible. You had to book two months in advance to dine in private homes where the very best food cooked in the very best manner was to be had. And believe me, none was better than Mrs. Hogg's in Gressingham. Our absolute favorite dining-in place, it always offered the identical meal, a creamy asparagus or leek soup, a precise quarter of the world's most exquisite roast duckling (I could have consumed an entire bird or two) served with sage and apple dressing, a big bowl of seasonal vegetables with fresh butter and a perfect trifle. Genial, small Mr. Hogg fed the ducks in the backyard from the evening's scraps and there never was a duckling more delicious, the skin crisp, dark brown standing right up from the flesh of the duck. Mrs. Hogg, a formidable, large woman who wore black men's socks with her heels and hot tweeds under her apron, though she had been roasting ten ducks, would never reveal how she got the skin to stand up and salute the diner or how she managed to banish any trace of fat.

Mrs. Hogg's trifle of fresh custard, raspberry preserves, sponge cake doused in sherry, and sprinkled with toasted coconut macaroons was served in individual little compotes with whipped cream. Lee flirted with her substantial self in order to get a second trifle, which always irritated me no end. You had to bring your own wine and Mr. Hogg uncorked it and placed too close to the fire, believing red should be warm and we never questioned his decision, for he needed all the assertion he could get. One had to be very well behaved at Mrs. Hogg's or you would not be welcomed, which we learned after bringing Galina Stovickova and her friends from Prague for dinner. It took Lee's persuasive flattery to get back into her good graces.

The fanciest restaurant in Morecambe was the Tropicana, all high 1950s chic with stained glass flamingoes and dark mahogany tables with throne-like chairs. It also featured duck, only this duck was not Mrs. Hogg's, but a whole half with skin firmly attached to the brown flesh. Because these ducks were raised in Gressingham or Derwentwater you could do little to ruin their taste, deliciously lying there next to the slice of orange and a maraschino cherry. I often roasted duckings and used a simple recipe, clove-stuck onions in the cavity, then sliced and served with Cumberland Sauce laced with brandy.

Austin Woolrych, the head of the History Department at the University and ever much the Little King, and his wife Muriel often entertained visiting professors and selected staff to dine at the Tropicana. One evening, when Keith Thomas was the (young) eminence grise, there erupted a heated discussion about the Shah of Iran, all deploring the obscene extravagance of the Peacock Throne Millennium in a miserably poor country, while Muriel defended his "sense of style" as we condescendingly stared up at the copper ceiling.

Another memorable Duck Night took place in Woodstock outside of Oxford during one of our annual overnights at the Stones who always spent the summer in their old home. Jeanne was an inspired cook and served one of the single best left over dishes I have ever eaten, wild rice sautéed in duck fat with sour cherries and some small shreds of the previous night's duck (served to more important houseguests, perhaps Dame Cecily Wedgwood!). Lawrence with his shirt buttons popped opened and the insouciant Academic Slouch had a fierce intensity and brilliance which gave Lee much needed inspiration isolated as he was in the backcountry. I thought Lawrence would have been Prime Minister had he gone into politics. What made him so intoxicating? The presence of power or the palpable tangible energy waves radiating from a fabulous mind?

The *Postgate Guides* that ranked restaurants were as cockamamie and unreliable as the food critics tormenting Basil in *Fawlty Towers* where the depiction of the social aspirations of the lower middle class to squirearchyhood was hilariously spot-on! Oh To Be A Gent! We had a lot of laughs when self-conscious pretension was observed at such restaurants as The Moor Cock in Clitheroe where atop a Bronte moor mysteriously quiet tuxedoed waiters padded around serving French wine and game pie to local publicans. Then there was always the fearful journey home on the unmarked roads. What if the car were to stop? What in the world would we do? This thought was always in mind when the sun set and the darkness became impenetrable with low cloud ceilings and starless black skies.

The would-be gents and their hairdo-ed wives were also spied at The Dairy in Kendal run by two "ladies who preferred ladies" who served ten courses, mainly a plethora of sorbets scattered throughout the long dinner. Here we celebrated our tenth wedding anniversary with pheasant stuffed with watercress, wrapped in bacon and served with wine gravy and the bird's tail feathers! Lee ate quickly counting the minutes on his Omega and the courses to get home for Match of the Day with Manchester United.

Two chicken dishes were frequent offerings chez Beier, both served cold, and perfect for buffet dinners. Coronation Chicken was featured at the deification of Queen Elizabeth II since it could withstand sitting out for a long while; a molded chicken salad with mayonnaise and cream, some curry and lemon, it was served chilled with green grapes and watercress and curry sauce. Then there was the classic Lancashire Hindle Wakes, which along with Lancashire clogs, were an inherent part of local culture. The dish was supposedly transported by Flemish weavers to the North but we do know a wake was a holiday week when the town factories were closed and Hindle an imaginary Lancashire town that appeared in a popular play first performed in 1912. Whatever fact or fiction, this was a festive dish to celebrate the temporary respite from work, a large chicken stuffed with prunes, almonds, herbs, simmered in water and malt vinegar and thickened with a lemon roux. Don't despair, it gets better the longer it simmers.

Still Life with Chocolate Cake, c. 1918 Roger Fry

With Pamela and Micu Diamand in the garden at Bouchernes

Russell Lawson in his kilt

Portrait of Arthur Waley by Roger Fry

Bushy in the bramble garden

Dairy cows lounging on the Cambridge greens

Penny Street, Lancaster

Lonsdale Tower at the University of Lancaster

Donny Adams in front of the Britannia

Lee surveys the troops during a demonstration

Tom Cahill and the Vicar of St. Mary's Priory give a trendy salute
watched by Lynn and Mick Murray

That's Ullswater in the distance

Long horned cattle watch as the fell walk starts.

A black tarn is in the lower left

A LAND OF SHEEP

In Northern England the sheep were to be contended with, running in great packs when the white fog suddenly descended on the moors and all you could see were misty black faces peering at you. Thankful at that moment they did not have the horns of the local longhorn cattle you always wondered if those scrappy black and white sheep dogs were around to corral them if they decided to charge. There are today an estimated three million sheep in Cumbria, mainly tough Herdwick stock originally brought over by the invading Norsemen and prized for staying on their own "heaf" or turf. Their brown, sturdy wool was exported from Whitehaven on the west coast of Cumberland to the Far East and the West Indies in exchange for those spices and sugar and rum featured in many local dishes. There were Sheep Meets held for hundreds of years, an annual occasion to return wandering sheep to their rightful owners, usually followed by a Tatie Pot dinner, a stew of lamb, black pudding and potatoes.

Local resident Beatrix Potter was chairman of the Herdwick Sheep Breeder's Association, though there is no evidence of fellow writers, those famous denizens of the Lake District, Wordsworth, Coleridge or Keats having had any particular interest in them. (I do recall an essay by Roger Fry in which he wonders if Wordsworth were reincarnated as a sheep.) Bred for their hardiness, they are today deemed a Heritage breed and highly prized in the fancy new food courts like Holker Hall in Cartmel. The hills and dales were strewn with the carcasses and bleached skulls of generations past; wool on barbed wire fencing was gathered by university wives who spun and wove it on antique looms and no fireplace was acceptable without a sheepskin rug. Among our first purchases up North were sturdy, heavy sheepskin jackets.

Since the Middle Ages sheep had been bred primarily for wool, the Wool Exchanges making England rich for centuries, but they were also the staple protein for Northerners. Today the open air stone structures where wool was traded are scattered throughout Northern towns like the engaging Alston in the North Pennines. Mutton disappeared from British menus after World War II and we certainly ate no two year olds but only the babies of the lot, Spring lamb—and it was almost always imported from Australia or New Zealand. The first refrigerated imports actually arrived from New Zealand in 1882, and by 1933 half of all British lamb was from Down Under, which remained the case until the end of the 1970s. Imported lamb declined in the 1980s as artisanal indigenous breeds became highly prized. A century of unrestricted imports food from the late 18th century and throughout the 19th had all but totally destroyed local food tradition and in the 1960s and 70s there was still near total dependence on foreign food imports.

Meat and potatoes appeared everywhere and in many guises in the North. Lancashire Hotpot, what could be more a synonym of Northern cooking?, as grim and earthy as the life of a sheepherder, was the standard lamb dish. Basically the same as Irish Stew it included potatoes and onions and perhaps carrots or turnips. Lancashire was the first English county to embrace the potato because it is closest to Ireland and potatoes were the standard vegetable of Lancashire growing readily in its temperate climate and deep mossy soil. In 1700 there was reference to a potato bed in that wet and windy place Garstang between Lancaster and Preston. Hotpot was named for the big steep sided crockery pot or pippin the lamb and potatoes and onions cooked in all day in the fireplace when the denizens were in the tin mines or in the fields or cotton and linen mills. It was the cuisine of poverty as noted by novelist Elizabeth Gaskell who tells a tale of the mill owner sharing the humble pot with his workers.

If pinched I used scrag's end neck of lamb, if a bit more flush, best end which was the meat behind the shoulder, with onions, potatoes, sometimes carrots and seasonings including brown sugar, thyme and mace. There are as many versions as there are people and sometimes Worcestershire sauce or tomato puree or bay leaves are added. One famous version is called Lobscouse and it hails from Liverpool and Merseyside, the word for sailor, labskause, in German. Brought to the seafaring towns of Western England from across the North Sea it combines stewing steak, as well as breast of lamb or scrag's end, the same veggies as a hotpot but with the addition of beer instead of the stock. Sailors added hard tack before serving no doubt to make the intractable biscuits edible. Patrick O'Brian celebrated the dish in his Aubrey and Maturin novels and the cookbook *Labscouse and Spotted Dog*.

Shepherd's Pie is composed of cooked stewing lamb or ground lamb (if beef is used it is always called Cottage Pie) sautéed with onions, thyme, Worcestershire, and topped with mashed potatoes, then sprinkled with Lancashire cheese. Cornish pasties were made with lamb not beef in the North and though they derive the name from the Southwest of England were present everywhere in Lancashire and Cumbria. Sometimes called Lancashire Foot, it was a portable food for the tin and coal miners whose dirty hands could grip the pastry handles, which were then discarded. One of my favorite dishes was Westmorland Lamb (or Sweet) Pie in which lamb is combined with apples, currants and other dried fruits, brown sugar, rum, nutmeg, cinnamon, mace all poured into shortcrust pastry. Melton Mowbray might have had its pork pies but lamb pies were Northern delights.

THE ROMANCE OF THE ROAST

On our fell walks we encountered big, free-roaming, long haired and very long horned cattle, brown and black, grazing ruminants with glistening coats eating gorse and green grasses instead of the indigestible corn in sickening feedlots in America. Visitors to England have a real Romance of Roast Beef, that icon of food nationalism with the Beefeaters a symbol of the culinary history of the country. It is true that beef was plentiful and cheap in Britain largely due to the advanced scientific husbandry of 18th century entrepreneurs and hence it was always meat rich compared to the Continent. We also ate imported Argentinian beef which was much cheaper.

In all our years in England, however, the standing rib roast we had at the Reitlinger Museum that Christmas was the sole time we ever dined on a big joint of a slaughtered animal on a domestic table. There were no whole legs of lamb or haunches of fresh pork or veal roasts and when meat did appear it was in Frenchified in stews and daubes made with wine, or with beer as in boeuf a la Flamande. I perfected stewed meat dishes such as Hungarian goulash, where I always used lard and the best quality sweet paprika obtainable. The leftovers were made into soup adding sauerkraut and potatoes, just like Smutny's in Vienna, where we spied Francis Haskell and his wife dining at the adjacent table. Not to worry, they did not recognize us.

Steaks were not prized by American visitors because they were too small and did not cover the plates; they were of thinner cut, not aged at all to tenderize, less marbled and fatty than American beef and often stringy or tough. "Beier's Good Food Guide" was published in *Lancaster Comment* and though written entirely by yours truly I was called "the wife of the author". After nostalgically pining for the good fare in France I note that "there are some places in Lancaster and vicinity where you can eat without fear of getting a piece of glass in your curry or a rusty nail in your soup", both rueful experiences based in fact.

I also reviewed The Fenwick Arms in the Lune Valley, mildly praising its steak fresh from the local abattoir off Newlands Road in Lancaster. At this woody, dark, quintessentially English inn, heavy on copper pots and pewter chargers, Vice Chancellor Charles Carter and his wee wife often dined, much to the snoopy delight of junior academics peering around oaken pillars. Visiting dignitaries were often invited to dinner there and I recall such occasions with Father Dan Berrigan after his packed lecture rousing the troops against the Vietnam War. Or Sviatoslav Richter, without his boyfriend whom he left in a Morecambe boarding house, who had just played two marvelous concerts. Or a flirtatious Alger Hiss, who had opined to a crowded audience of skeptical students, about Richard Nixon. I wrote in my journals,

November 11, 1971

Last night Alger Hiss gave a talk on McCarthyism at the University-a gaunt small headed WASP sooooooooo proud of his Eastern Establishment Episcopalian background. He waxed lyrical about Eleanor's culture and humanity and he obviously loathed McC. himself like the low broad loathsome toad he undoubtedly was. I asked the question about parallels between the University and McCarthyism and Hiss answered everything evasively and obliquely. His lack of directness startling. He even refused outright to say anything bad about Nixon because he believed in the old adage that Americans should say nothing negative about their country's present politics when abroad. As if Alger Hiss were being more holy

American than thou. He said that the American people would not let the government get away with McC. today—pathetically naïve. What really frightened him about the Red Scare was the mass hysteria & lack of reason of all "good well-bred people. Hmmmmmmmmm". In retrospect I guess he was talking about himself.

A Bit of Cheese

English dairy cows were omnipresent, lounging on the psychedelic green lawns around Cambridge or roaming the hills and dales of the Lake District. Their milk was made into the world's best hard cheeses, sharp Cheddar, mellow Cheshire, creamy, complex Double Gloucester, ancient Wensleydale, Derby without the sage, and crumbly, tart, snow white Lancashire mentioned in the Doomsday Book. Then there was of course the King of All Cheeses, creamy Stilton, blue or white, made farther south. The North was true dairy country with fine pasture in the valleys. In the old stone farmhouses traditional Lancashire cheese was still made, quickly, aged only three weeks to satisfy immediate hunger. There was older "tasty" Lancashire aged up to nine months but we rarely ate this more expensive and sharper version.

A preserved food like candied orange peel or smoked herring, it was not necessary to keep cheese in a fridge, not that anyone had one. A cool larder in an unheated house worked just fine, thank you. Lancashire cheese was very mild, often unpasteurized, and perfect for Welsh rarebits (rabbits) because it melted so easily; combined with local bitters and dried mustard it was served over buttered toast. A fancier rabbit for guests consisted of Stilton and ale warmed together with breadcrumbs, Worcestershire and mustard, cooked slowly to a fine paste, to which was added an egg and Tabasco were added. This is great over pork chops and sautéed leeks or bread. Another favorite was Cheese and Onion Pie, crumbled Stilton or Lancashire combined with onions sautéed in butter and baked in shortcrust pastry.

Besides Cornish pasties and pickled onions, cheese was a staple of pub food as in a Ploughman's Lunch, chunks of Cheddar and Double Gloucestershire, gherkins or pickled onions and mustard with thickly sliced bread. Branston Pickle was also a usual accompaniment. Crosse & Blackwell sells a good version but I enjoyed making my own on a rainy afternoon with the fire flickering in the kitchen's large walk-in fireplace, and its reddish flagstone floors, marble topped pine cabinets (we got the marble from tombstone maker's rejects) and French doors opening on to the untended garden. I chopped into small cubes carrot, turnip or rutabaga, dates, onion, apple, zucchini, gherkins, cauliflower flowerets and added garlic, brown sugar, lemon, apple cider, a spot of allspice, Worcestershire and Coleman's mustard. After simmering for two hours Kitchen Bouquet was added for color and all this concoction placed into sterilized jars. It had to sit several weeks in the fridge before it was just right. It is absolutely divine with Lancashire cheese.

PIGS IN CUMBERLAND

Pigs proliferated in the North and resonant of the old county name, Cumberland hams were dry cured, rubbed with salt and brown sugar and unsmoked. Sweet, porcine, delicious. We took large slices on those eight hour hikes and rambles, keeping them separate from the grainy bread and assembling the sandwich, topped with whole grain mustard, sitting on a cairn overlooking Ullswater or Coniston Water. For nightly dinner I occasionally sautéed gammon in butter, raw pork from the rear haunches of a pig it was only very slightly cured. Then there was ubiquitous bacon, always imported from Denmark, that exquisite smoked pork loin with a nice fatty tail.

Cumberland sausage was large and snowy white, mild and completely untreated with chemical additives, just fresh pork shoulder, a bit of smoked bacon or pork belly, very few breadcrumbs and all seasoned with salt, black pepper, nutmeg and mace. They appeared in large coils in the windows of every butcher shop and were irresistible, served with home-made Cumberland Sauce of red currant jelly, mustard and whatever booze on hand, port or Madeira or brandy or red wine. Sauce could also be made with Damson jam and with a pinch of cinnamon it was also perfect with local venison or lamb.

I used Cumberland sausage in cassoulets along with best end of lamb cooked in a garlicky tomato sauce and chicken that was smoked right on Glasson Dock where you could also bring your woodcock or Lune salmon to get the treatment. Today with the artisanal food revolution in full swing, it is called The Port of Lancaster Smokehouse. The meats were added to white navy beans and covered with a thick bread crust and the resulting cassoulet was good as any French version. I served this for a sit down party for fourteen when we were living in Cockerham along with our homemade beer. The dinner, and I remember it like it was yesterday, was a perfect cassoulet cooked in a large Creuset red casserole, preceded by soupe au pistou and crudites with aioli and Bushy delivering a live vole from the garden which got loose under the long table. Dick Frost complained that the beer was "weak piss" then passed out after drinking several glasses on the bed upstairs.

Best Bitters

For a whole year we experimented with beer making in our damp basement reeking of creosote to discourage voracious Northern termites. What a production, but then again we had a lifetime ahead of us to worry about time, as we shopped for barley, hops and malt in a special shop in the Lake District and spent entire weekends mashing and draining and siphoning and adding finings and bottling from the big yellow plastic bins. It was not only a laborious activity but a powerful and inexpensive way to get a buzz; we were often so anxious to try it we couldn't wait the requisite two weeks for proper fermentation. We had stomachs of iron in our twenties.

In Lancaster fine beer meant Mitchell's or Yates and Jackson bitters. A crisis hit the breweries in the late 60s when the large nationals began acquiring or closing down smaller, regional ones. We were livid when they abandoned the practice of serving ale from kegs opting for a cheaper system of filtered, pasteurized beers. Many joined CAMRA which is still flourishing with its mission to protect real beer. We were so proud of Yates & Jackson which had been in Lancaster since 1669; it was bought by Thwaites several years after we left in 1984 and local ale masters lament that the beer is not what it was and I am sure it is not. Mitchell's of Lancaster is still one of the few independent beer companies in Britain, God Bless Them. When in Manchester we drank Boddington and in the Lakes Jennings Brothers, companies founded 200 years ago and still brewing fine stout, bitter, porter and ales. We lovers of live fermenting beer deeply frowned on Watney's Red Label or Tetleys.

Live beer was served in the pubs which had greatly restricted hours, another sign of working class oppression, so the Lord Ashtons could be assured the laborers would be fit as fiddles to put in another 14-hour day in the mills. The gents belonged to private clubs where they could drink all day and night if they so desired and the working class had their working men's clubs, which were however slowly fading away in the 70s. Local pubs attracted a few academics, though most of the latter preferred to stay at Bailrigg and drink with members of their own department. There is no more arcane conversation than in this tiny world of infighting and pedantry where the smaller the stakes the more vicious the verbiage. That is so English—talking and acting our aggressions by word of mouth not fists. I often thought if Americans talked to one another or about one another the ways the blokes do there would be bodies scattered everywhere.

After a day in Preston I could not wait to hit the Britannia Hotel or Freeholder's Arms and order a large cold draught, first a lager, which I drank in one gulp, then a coupla Yates. I don't think there was anything else in the bar except some scotch, an old piano and a dartboard. The local lads, descended from the Vikings, were rugged and handsome and so different from the university types. Once I went for a pint with our carpenter (trying another method of exterminating termites), Joe Richmond, whom I adored because he called me "flower" a common epithet which to my ears sounded romantic; Lee didn't seem to mind but when I drove Joe back to his Council House his wife would not let him in, screamed the way only those who lived in the perpetual vernacular do, and Joe had to sleep in the bus station. A favorite university joke was, they don't bury the dead in Lancaster, they stand them up in the bus station.

The women sat off to the right in a side room at tables smoking Winstons, drinking shandys, eating egg salad sandwiches and occasionally getting up to sing a song. When my adorable mother visited she was unstoppable at the piano which embarrassed Lee; my equally adorable mother-in-law Janet LaVerne loved to drink scotch in the pubs, always complaining about the utter and final lack of ice, and richly conspicuous in her Burberry plaids, golden bracelets, cashmere sweaters and ropes of amber. In England one assumed protective camouflage when outdoors, or indoors for that matter, perhaps the third characteristic of all classes being a relative indifference to appearance. It took years to get reacquainted with American consumer mania and obsession with owning twenty sweaters instead of two.

TEATIME

Tea in Lancaster was not tea at Derry and Tom's in London; it was not the rich man's 4:00 fancy teacake tea that foreigners sought out nor was it the 6:00 High Tea or supper that the working classes ate. Everyone drank the livelong day. The gentry ate dinner at 7:30 and called it dinner as did those professionals like professors, doctors, solicitors, retired colonels and ghurkas, who had attended Rugby or Winchester then Oxford or Cambridge or the LSE. Now they retreated into country life where they could live in little castles like Hornby in Kirby Lonsdale or 17th century farmhouses and tried to live the fantasy life of an English gentleman. I think every barber and publican and certainly quite a few professorial types wanted to be lairds of a Highland croft or a manor house and would name their bungalows Shangri-La omitting the street numbers in the suburban sprawl.

The North abounded with the aspirations of small squiredom, and you could observe this when wives took daily tea, selecting the venue appropriately. There were two tea shops directly across the street from each other and both charged precisely 10 pence per cup, but the one establishment served it in flowered porcelain cups with saucers and fine scones with Devonshire clotted cream; the other shop served tea in thick white mugs with a slab of parkin or barm bread with lemon curd.

Tea, its continual sweetened consumption, in a cold, damp land is a matter of healthy survival since it warmed you from the inside when there was no heat except perhaps a faint coal fire in the grate. There was no ritual associated with drinking tea, which was served everywhere, all day, all the time, with milk and sugar and certainly never lemon. Lancashire ladies always watched to see if you put the milk in before or after you poured the tea to see where you belonged in the social hierarchy.

My friend Stella Longland heiress to the Brook Bond tea fortune, like so many upper class girls had a fascination with the occult and the underclass. She lived with a local Hell's Angel called Edge (real name Wilfred Lamb) who like his fellow members in Lancaster could not afford a motorcycle and not much more than black leather jackets and tattoos. He looked violent but was as sweet as his real name suggested and eventually Stella bought him a Vespa.

ELIZABETH DAVID

I bought the Penguin paperback editions of Elizabeth David's books reprinted from the originals of the 1950s, *Mediterranean Food, Italian Food, French Country Cooking* and *Summer Cooking.* Those evocative line drawings of John Minton and the enchanting recipes transported me to the South, the South of anywhere *not* Lancaster with rich tastes from what Marius the Epicurean called lands of various sunshine! I cooked many, so many of the recipes, happy there were no tedious measurements, just cups and spoons and splashes, and the outcome was so much more delicious than those of Childean didacticism. I could willfully overdo an herb or the amount of wine or oil because I was not going to measure my life with Prufrockian teaspoons!

Julia Child found Elizabeth David's books unprofessional though when they met in the 1960s they purportedly became friends; both had worked in intelligence abroad from their respective countries in WW II and both were very affluent, well connected upper middle class lasses. Unlike the alluring and adventurous Elizabeth, given a rather distasteful shake in Artemis Cooper's indiscreet biography, Julia's charm derived from the fact she was such a square, with her odd appearance and impossible voice. She had the great good fortune to find a devoted handmaiden in Paul, rather like Leonard Woolf was to Virginia.

A sort of mirror image of Elizabeth David lived several thousand miles away and was of the same generation. M.F.K. Fisher was not a cookbook writer but the creator of a genre where the gustatory experience was the protagonist. She also had experienced wartime stringency in the kitchen but the recipes in *How to Cook a Wolf* were decidedly not Mediterranean but English- American, shrimp, pates, and eggs with anchovies and soups reminding me so much of the economies I practiced in England. I always envied her vastly uninhibited nature and the places it took her in life.

NOTHING REFINED PLEASE

In 1967 Edmund Leach's Reith lectures damned fast food and frozen food equating them with that particularly English form of Protestant guilt, moral turpitude. The first age of macrobiotics, when Prince Charles noticed that all was not well with the culinary kingdom, also caught our wary, gimlet eyes. Then along came Roger Williams' *Nutrition Against Disease* which proved our food philosophy was right: nothing white, no white bread, no white sugar, no white pasta, no white potatoes and certainly no white rice. We followed this regime for about six months until it became a tasteless chore but for a time bread was strenuously whole wheat, the more whole the better, rice very brown, potatoes sweet and orange hued, sugar as dark as Hades or at least Demerara. Lee of course had to have his weekly favorite so we made an exception. Garlic spaghetti consisted of sweating five to ten sliced garlic cloves in olive oil, removing them, then pouring the fragrant oil over steaming spaghetti, dried oregano and red pepper flakes, then all sprinkled with Parmesan from the jar. When you think about it this could be the world's finest dish.

Lee made bread that was exactly like Postlethwaite's, the wheat ground by hand before our very eyes and the final loaf served with fresh comb honey we went great distances over hill and dale to obtain. Our home-made yogurt, the offspring of a mother culture that was used time and again, quietly fermented on the Aga and was sourly perfect with the sweet honey. Tom Cahill from Grosse Point, Michigan and sundry other malcontents kept bees at their commune, Badger's Gate, where food seemed to be the main preoccupation, besides the opposite sex and marijuana which they also grew. There was a goat for milk, cabbage patches, oceans of peanut butter, not to mention millet bread and bread with other odd grains. I felt it such a waste of ambition to be consumed with the minutiae of life but this group seemed to curiously lack ambition probably from smoking weed though they claimed it was depression about Capitalism and Vietnam. Everything was eco this and eco that and organic fertilizer and alternative energy was imperative on progressive communes where money never seemed to be a problem.

It looked like we could stop the Vietnam War so we could certainly stop disease. We were rarely ill and when we were it was catastrophic. No nutrition could have prevented the scarring of my Fallopian tubes and the ectopic pregnancy that would have spelt death half a century earlier. Dr. Patrick Steptoe, two years away from Louise Brooks and the first successful in vitro fertilization, agreed to treat my infertility on National Health in his Oldham, Lancashire office. When he told us to forget it, we would never have children, the first thing I wanted was a pizza and a bottle of wine to dull the absolutely excruciating pain but Lee had to get home to count those sturdy beggars on their way to Devil's Arse A Peak, Derbyshire.

Whenever life has thrown an ugly unbearable curve ball, say after my brother's untimely death, my first thought has always been pizza and wine or meatballs and spaghetti and wine. When my old Cadillac broke down and I was utterly alone in Bryce Canyon in a January snowstorm, I hitched a ride with a total stranger who thankfully was Bob Fisher the Mayor of Carson City, Nevada. Back in god-awful Green River, the fan belt was fixed and I drove through the night to Las Vegas. I pulled into the first place with a neon light and ordered meatballs and spaghetti and a bottle of wine, at 4 A.M. It was perhaps the most glorious meal I have ever had since I was brought back from the dead—and Utah!

COOKING FOR THE PROFESSORS

Food had that ceremonial social function it had had in Princeton, especially when at Lee's behest I cooked for the professors. Doing so ensured that a mere lecturer's status on the academic ladder was upped a rung or two, especially when that lecturer was labeled a radical troublemaker. When you cook a feast basic anthropology supercedes politics. Professors or Readers from one's own department would greedily accept an invitation knowing the restaurants were execrable and one needed to book Hodge Hill or Sharrow Bay at least two months in advance. In-home entertaining was the only game in town.

When we divorced a decade later that entire system, the structure that meals offered to my existence utterly dissolved and my food habits and culinary experience reflected a new reality, fast, rootless, sporadic, deeply unceremonious, on the run. But that was all to come, now witherslacks made great jam and Seville oranges great marmalade and Blue Mountain coffee and Lapsang Souchong were perfection and I had to cook for Austin Woolrych and Harold Perkin and their wives.

Harold, the second in command in the History Department, was a working class lad and like so many academics who had made it into a (perceived) higher echelon, he combined a defiant cocksureness with a deep sense of inferiority, defensively pouncing on any suggestion of class snobbery, yet snobbishly aping the gentry in clothing and home and horses. Alas Harold and Joan's Pottery's twang would betray any efforts at social climbing and although he hated the campus radicals who so championed his own working class, (we preferred the honesty and class solidarity of

E.P. Thompson and Raymond Williams) our seriously groaning board dissipated his anger somewhat.

I proofread the first draft of his MS for *The Origins of Modern British Society* and thought it festooned with mixed metaphors and not enough statistics to prove his broad statements. It went on to become a classic in the field probably because he dared to make those generalizations, not unduly burdened with the mind numbing footnotes and other paraphernalia of history writing. Years later long after my divorce I was invited to dinner chez Perkin in Evanston, Illinois when he was visiting professor at Northwestern. The dinner was as frugal with the same first course of eggs and anchovies and a slice of ham with two veggies as if Joan were cooking at their 17th century Caton farmhouse. She seemed so out of context, so lonely for England, a sentiment this expatriate knew well. It all has something to do with having played the same games in childhood and eaten the same breakfast cereals.

Austin, a Civil War scholar who had written some slim volumes about Cromwell, was a brooding solitary figure, a melancholy soul who liked to walk the moors alone. I loved his old school military demeanor, uncomfortable stuffiness and powerful class consciousness. He was a benevolent if nervous host to the feisty and disrespectful young faculty he had assembled for his department and with his wife Muriel, who told us a thousand times she had seen the Prince of Wales riding near her Berkshire home, often had us over to *his* 17th century Caton farmhouse for departmental parties. Just departmental mind you since we were junior staff and formal protocol was, well, formal protocol. Did we know that Dame this or that, or Asa Briggs or Christopher Hill or Eric Hobsbawm, or J.H. Plumb or Geoffrey Elton or other illuminati had recently sat on the very chairs on which we were sitting? Austin had once sold mens' shirts in Harrods because his father had gone bust in the Great Depression as the snide lecturers constantly tittered about. Their house was stuffed with antiques and Muriel's collection of Victorian card cases framed in velvet on the walls.

They were the bi-annual recipients of an outrageous, overblown Beier Meal, a notable one being Mishmishya, a Claudia Roden recipe of lamb, almonds and apricots which created the evening's guess what's in the pot entertainment. After dinner and the green salad always served after the meal a la francais (we sneered at those who ate it first!) I set out a cheese platter of both blue and white Stilton, Camembert, Port Salut, accompanied by pears poached in red wine. Then a savory, the old standby Scotch Woodcock, then cakes and tarts and After Eight mints with the vintage Armagnac we smuggled back from France under the front seat of the Morris Minor that the locals called the jam jar. I always cheerfully accepted the laborious commitment because cooking and reading cookbooks was for me as much entertainment as the apotheosis of the whole affair, the arrival of the guests.

The head of the Poli Sci Department and later VC of the University, Philip Reynolds and his wife Molly were as chic as an academic couple could ever possibly be. In their townhouse in the city, decidedly non-17th century-farmhouse, and a breath of fresh air from Belgravia, they threw a dinner party to which we were invited. A visibly shaken Austin actually gasped when he saw a mere lecturer and his wife in the living room, which did not, however, seem to phase the university psychiatrist. Dr. Theobald (pronounced Tibbald) who had greater concerns, namely preventing students from jumping off Lonsdale Tower. Thoroughly clean of any interest in Freud or Jung or Karen Horney, whom I was reading at the time to figure out what was wrong with my marriage, his main interest was the sherry. Molly who smoked incessantly and put the butts out in a Ming vase suggested a spot of whiskey instead of fino before dinner, Austin sneered at this gauche American habit which spurred me to have two spots after which smelling salts were needed for my revival. After canned consommé dollied up with chives there was a well known dish, Partridge Jubilee, or small birds, probably pigeons since academics were parsimonious, browned in butter to which cherries, Madeira, sugar, and lemon were added, then served over toast with a slice of pate on top.

Philip knavishly recounted how he told the eminent historian Basil Liddell-Hart that Montgomery was the biggest clown on the stage of World War II only to be faced by a blank stare and a mumble that indeed they had been fast friends. This was a big story in the remote monastery that was Academia, but Dr. Theobald remained glassy eyed and Molly continued to put out butts in the Ming vase until her husband erupted and in solidarity I did the same and Lee did not talk to me for days since the social code, even for a left-wing socialist, was somehow breached.

SUNDERLAND POINT

The University sculptor-in-residence, John Hoskins, a dead ringer for the Stone Age likes of Henry Moore, like so many artists craved isolation to better create huge strange objects that expressed their takes on the world. What a demanding career choice. Sunderland Point was about as inaccessible a place as you could get except for the Outer Hebrides or Faroe Islands, and it was here John and his second wife Doreen chose to live. Discovered and settled by a Quaker businessman Robert Lawson, it saw the very first shipment of cotton from the American South arrive in the 18th century.

At Sunderland Point was a remarkable sight, Sambo's Grave, where on unconsecrated ground, in 1736 a slave was buried on the cold sandy bay so far from home. The headstone reads:

Here lies

Poor Sambo

A Faithful Negro

Who

Attending his master from the Weft Indies

Died on his arrival in Sunderland

After the American Civil war no more cotton and no more slaves were shipped to Lancashire and it was the beginning of the end of the hundred-year empire of King Cotton in the North of England.

Overlooking Morecambe Bay, when the tide came in, the tiny village was completely cut off from the town of Overton and became an island for twelve hours every day of the year. It was a dash to arrive before the rushing tide, since visits were always timed so we would have to outrun it on the narrow road over the salt marsh. Once we had to abandon the jam jar and scramble up slopes while the waters consumed the little vehicle and we strode the high ground to the Hoskin's dinner table. The meals were long and boozy (Thank God for artists!) and we always slept on the sofa for the night.

Doreen like so many women at the time were self-conscious Earth Mothers, warm, nurturing, deeply unadventurous and tied by the apron strings to hearth and home though they probably questioned the wisdom of that role when their husbands ran off with their students. I was far too cynical to buy that claptrap, besides I had itchy feet and wanted to see the rest of the world, or at least more than a tiny plot of earth in the water.

SUSAN'S SAUCE

Susan Bassnet McGuire, reared in Rome, was a feminist member of the English Department and a blond, prettier Germaine Greer whom she knew—and respected—at the University of Warwick. Susan often made a communal dish, like my "Sicilian" mussels or Lancaster Cassoulet, an unusual spaghetti sauce, which I have never seen anywhere else. Into olive oil went chopped Danish bacon and chopped green peppers, garlic and tomatoes, red pepper flakes, dried oregano, all this cooked for hours and hours and hours as we sat around, drank wine and talked about the medieval-minded university administration and the prevalence of the Business University Carter was creating. Or we would recount tales of recent travels to Greece or Spain or Minorca or Kenya or Russia, never fully conscious of the disparity between our privileged lives and the chip and butty eaters we idealized, eking out a living down the road.

Today I guess you would call it Bohemian Chic, but we wouldn't have since we were truly going to help "the workers" and change British society. I helped organize the Claimant's Union for souls on the Dole but soon discovered all they really wanted was a warmer coat and extra food and not a movement. They could not, probably wisely, give one tu'penny damn about ideas. I find it amusing to note that one of the most vociferous protestors of the time Marion McClintock is still an administrator in the English Department at the University of Lancaster. She, who had demonstrated about sex discrimination with Susan, has written a book about the period 1964-74 at the University called a *Quest for Innovation.* So strange is memory since I remember her as a fierce anti-establishment camarade with her fey husband Peter.

THE PARSIMONIUS ENGLISHMAN

This was the era of Duke for A Day where the so-named would invite you to dine chez eux or stay the night for a pretty penny to pay the estate taxes. We experienced similar parsimony or penuriousness in many English homes at the time, some friends actually halving eggs for breakfast and serving the half with half a piece of shortbread. Roger Smith and his wife Lydia, thin, anemic, nervous lived in Austwick in an old stone farmhouse where they escaped from her deep phobia for barking dogs only to find a beagle farm right over the hill. She was from Wisconsin and had met Roger in Whitby while a student and her meals were Barthesian signifiers of her Weltanschauung, her Zeitgeist, large boiled animal tongues with dried mustard powder diluted with water, potatoes with butter, salt and pepper, boiled vegetables, maybe some cider. It was during one of these dour meals that I decided I had to leave England. There *had* to be light and cheer somewhere in the world.

At a quaint tiny cottage in Wray next to the local pub, a scant cheese fondue pot was provided for six hungry guests by Michael Argles the university Librarian, all 6'6 of him and his fourth wife Jean. With his Eton/ Christ Church background Michael had nothing to prove to anyone after all. Other guests were Emlyn Lloyd and his German wife Frieda (foreign wives were then what trophy wives or Oriental wives are today) and a fortunately fat vicar and wife who scarfed up nuts and dried apricots after dinner. Lee and I went to get a breath of air and ran into the pub and wolfed down a pastie or two. Jean was forgiven because her father Colonel Owtram opened his manse and fine gardens on Sundays for champagne breakfasts after church, an unusual ritual for the non-religious English. Then the Colonel discovered that he could get away with charging guests to see the gardens and could never understand why no one wanted to drink champagne anymore on Sunday mornings. Parsimony was also a sign of superiority, a sort of noblesse oblige, no desire to go too much out of one's way for anyone.

Ineffably charming Joe Shennan, another unnaturally tall and thin Englishman, was Senior Lecturer in the History Department. An intelligence officer during the War, he was guardian of highly classified documents which were protected under heavy iron lock and key, until one day he noted the back of the file cabinet was made of cardboard. His wife Margaret, no slave to fashion, considered dinner to be cucumber and watercress sandwiches, which shocked me since we had exercised no such restraint when entertaining them with five courses. We were given our due considering our station—a junior lecturer and wife. Who cared! It was a good excuse to leave early and hit the local pubs before they closed at 10:00.

AMERICANS ABROAD

Bob and Paulette Bliss, both from Iowa, were always late which was taboo in structured Beier Time. One Thanksgiving I cooked a beautiful wild turkey that was the most delicious I have ever made, before or since, but alas at the last minute the wife had a headache, or an invitation to a better party. So that's what happened to the democratic spirit, those middle class liberals really just wanted an invitation to one of those gigantic lawn parties at Buckingham Palace or to a solicitor's 19th century castle in Kirby Lonsdale. When one cancelled on the same day without sufficient notice you scrambled to find a replacement from that list of hungry bachelors like Al Cohan from Miami. Al was my first gay friend and I discovered the wit, humor, not to mention great cooking, of all my subsequent male friends. What I have not figured out is why I always prefer gay guys to women (of any stripe) as friends.

Lancaster University attracted many American academics like the Bliss' or Barry Schutz or Al Cohan or Tom Cahill, spiritual refugees from Vietnam Amerika but more probably more accurately just lured there by Charles Carter. A devout Quaker, a statistician, enamored of business and technology he must have rued his policy many many times. The Americans were always heavily involved in the campus' anti war folderol, the protests against government policy in Northern Ireland (how many Bloody Sunday events did we attend) and all the sit ins and write ins and strikes and union organizing. I invited the Black Panthers to Northwest England, and they sent a Nigerian student from London who delivered a fiery speech which I ecstatically praised in *Lancaster Comment*. I also wrote a play about the prison life of George Jackson, Soleded Brother, but attempts to produce it on campus came to naught when Pakistani students did not make convincing American blacks.

Maria Schutz was of Mexican descent and had almost completed her law degree, but taking care of Barry was a full time occupation as his wild emotionalism and LSD trips in the Lakes could have driven a lesser person mad. Maria taught me to make authentic chili or as authentic as that era knew of, dried red beans boiled forever and added to fried onions, garlic, tinned tomatoes, minced beef all cooked for an hour. At the very end she added a large piece of dark chocolate, a pinch of cinnamon and served it all with rice that had been fried in garlic and oil until dark brown. I served this in my dining room with the red oilcloth on the oaken refectory table, old Blue Willow on the walls and blue and white chevron striped drapes, such a patriotic combination of colors. In these years there were no salsas or even ideas of what salsa was, no cilantro, very few sightings of avocado but sour cream and grated cheddar. Barry and Maria went to Rhodesia and wrote me many letters shocked at how she was treated as a black person. They later had a daughter they named Evita.

We met many American GIs—and Vanessa Redgrave—while attending anti-war rallies in Cambridge and London. They were organized by PEACE, (People Emerging Against Corrupt Establishments) which the actress, fresh from Isadora Duncan fame, funded as well as its newspaper intended to rouse the American GIs stationed at RAF bases against the war. In her *Autobiography* Redgrave recalls, "With two English friends and some Rhodes scholar graduate students at Cambridge I began to organize a GI anti-war newspaper PEACE." She also remembers that the two biggest USAF bases were Bentwaters and Mildenhall where Lee and I leafleted regularly and met with American GIs though there really were only a handful who were activists. The benefit at the Lyceum which was filmed by Harlech TV was attended by us and two dozen or so others to gain publicity for the Culver Case a court martial cause celebre. Many of the so-called GIs were spies or plants but I remember most fondly the camaraderie and the many pizzas I made for them in our kitchen at 35 Bishops Road, Highgate that year Lee decided to get involved seriously in the anti-war effort.

Vanessa had a brother Corin who was truly radical, recruiting followers to a compound where brainwashing supposedly took place. The era was full of sectarian gossip and finger pointing and I was called a Stalinist by some far left groups for wanting to help "the people" and hence "support the system". These academics really thought they were creating a revolution but it was all just talk in the end, effective talk but talk. The infighting from sects within PEACE was so scholastic I slipped out of meetings to sunbathe with Jane Egan in Cambridge and talk about how to raise funds for Survival International which was trying to preserve Brazilian Indians in the rapidly depleted rainforests. I hate to think of what it is like today and the Indian children are probably in the barrios of Sao Paolo.

I felt overwhelming nostalgia for the wide open spaces and the food of the States when visiting RAF base commissaries, a land of Wheaties not Weetabix. We had after all not gone home for seven years. After the pow wows we went to Anwar's Chat Patta on Tottenham Court Road for fiery Indian cooking, the Kathi Kebab making GIs gasp, grab a beer then grin from ear to ear. Food, nostalgia, the War, Anwar's, the tomb of Marx in Highgate Cemetery, Spike Milligan, all were one experiential continuum and are today an almost palpable memory.

THE ROBIN DAY OF BOMBAY

In the 1960s Indians were expelled from Uganda and Kenya and many went to England and opened restaurants. Lancaster had not of course attracted the best but those in London were a revelation. I always found the Indians and Pakistanis charming and delightful and felt so sorry for the fact they had to appear so anxious to please despite the discrimination. Our friend Sue Dawson, an architect who actually swooned when looking at houses, lived with a graduate student at Lancaster, Kunwar Sinha, once a popular broadcaster in Bombay.

When Lee and Sue and the Dalmatian Huckleberry hiked the unspeakably bleak terrain around Botton Head, which at 1488 feet is the highest peak in the north Yorkshire moors (that malevolent place), in the cottage kitchen with the wood burning stove the Robin Day of Bombay and I took refuge from the rain and fog and gloom. Ken (his English name) taught me how to cook Southern Indian style over the course of a year, lessons no books or TV programs could ever replicate, not pretentious, not fancy, no grinding of spices from scratch but a curry powder assembled from twice the amount of coriander and turmeric as cumin, a bit of powdered ginger and cayenne, and at the very end right before serving a hearty teaspoon of garam masala.

First Ken sautéed onions and garlic in clarified butter then added the curry mixture which fried carefully for a few minutes. In went yogurt boiling rapidly until a paste was formed, then skinned chicken pieces were added, covered with water and cooked for an hour. It was served with basmati rice cooked Indian style, the bottom of a saucepan coated with clarified butter, the washed rice added as well as a scant inch of water above the rice, boiled for half a minute then the lid put on with a dishtowel under it. It was taken off the heat and never touched again until ready to serve with its glorious golden crust formed on the bottom. Ken's curry was served with mango chutney and the most divine oily, green, and very hot lime pickle to which we were addicted.

If cooking beef or lamb the procedure was identical except you added tomatoes instead of yogurt. For vegetable dishes like eggplant and potatoes or cabbage and green pepper you could add cardamom, fennel seeds, caraway and other spices and omit the garam masala. I always tried to color coordinate my menu say a yellow chicken dish, a greenish lamb and spinach, a red, a white, perhaps orange.

Today I think Indian food all tastes very uniform, good, bad, rich, poor, north, south. In the end, curry is curry and overpowers anything added to it, fish or fowl or flora though there may be variation of spice overtones, heat, sharpness, or sweetness or texture. I have cooked many of Madhur Jaffrey's recipes and my favorite is the Mock Tandoori Chicken but when in the mood for curry has always reverted to Ken's technique. In New York I recently ate at the Kaluystan Café and wanted to yell to the chefs to please not try to make Indian cooking nouveau and beautifully dished up like a painting; go to the Jackson Heights Diner if you really want good old curry buffet.

ANTIBES

No place in the world is more beautiful than Antibes. Nowhere. OK maybe Capri. In August 1968 the student rebellion at the Odeon in Paris the previous spring emptied out the Cote d'Azur, for once somewhat free from tourists. We stayed at a little pension with a magnificent garden, Les Coquelicots, named for those delicious bright red poppies as in the Monet painting. Located right on the Cap within sight of the Grimaldi Castle, pink against the aquamarine sea and the golden ramparts, I yearned to stay forever, rent a studio and write novels like Lawrence Durrell. Drinking red wine, smoking Gauloises Maryland, and falling in love were also part of the fantasy scenario.

The weather was a caress, the Mediterranean mesmerizing, the drives to Vallauris to buy pink and blue pottery that mysteriously became orange and green in England, enchanting, and the food at the little hotel simple but sublime. My mother joined us and she and Lee became warriors in the battle for the food that graced the wooden table in the garden, eyeing everything to the last sliver of roasted garlic, the final haricot or chicken scrap, simultaneously stabbing the remains on the serving plates. It was not hunger but resentment, a small tear that became a chasm since that honeymoon in Ireland when she joined us and . . . well you know how mothers feel about their daughters and the selfish men who take them away all too soon. Food signifies not only character but ideology; look at what and how a person eats with others and you have a graph of character. Some offer you the plate first, some anxiously grab the best piece, some share, and, horror of horrors, some hold the knife and fork as if they are barbarians wielding pitchforks.

I have never replicated the flavor, the texture, anything at all about the elusive quality of the haricot verts with tomatoes, lavender thyme and fresh garlic in the olive oil of Provence though I tried dozens of time. There is a distinct terroir in all produce as well as in the grapes that make wine and perhaps you can only appreciate the food of France, or anywhere else in the world, when it is fresh from the soil. Or perhaps only after you have spent years living on the 55th parallel when the cells in your body scream out for sun and light like a plant kept too long in the dark. I always brought Roger Fry's *Cezanne* or *Vision and Design* to the South of France luxuriating in the sun and in the idea of living what I thought was the right kind of existence. On one trip I visited Marie, the widow of Charles Mauron, a great friend of Fry's as eccentric an aesthetician as you can imagine, in their farmhouse in St. Remy but alas there are no culinary memories since a BBC crew was lurking outside to talk to her about Bloomsbury. It had been officially discovered!

THE GIRARDOT OF ST. MAX

Lee met Alain Girardot and his wife Michelle in Nancy during that year he collected the Daum and the damask and the data about revolutionary France. They were true Lorrainers very tall with Gallic faces and the stature of Germans, les sals boches they loathed. Staying in their small townhouse in the suburb of Nancy, St. Max, we went on Roman digs and shopped for food and went to cafes and ate and ate and ate, Lee always whispering to me something about the enduring peasant origins of France.

On Christmas Eve 1968 we visited Michelle's grandparents on a tiny farm to the south of the city, where they had survived for eighty years in a small cottage with dirt floors and a fireplace as in Van Gogh's *Potato Eaters*. Outside were farmyard animals, a vegetable patch with mirabelle bushes and a still for fermenting the yellow berries. A fat turkey with a tiny head and a huge body had been pampered for the Christmas feast, raised in an ideal world of delicious scraps from the table, probably a little vin rouge as well, its life happy and indulged, its demise swift and painless. We need not even mention how the poor animals are raised today; we blame the necessity of demographics but there are humane options.

The preparation for the Christmas Eve feast started the 23rd when we made a rhum au baba to soak for two days. In the next 24 or 36 hours Michelle and I shopped and shopped for food, peeled and roasted chestnuts, she defeathering several small faisans for a Babette's Feast, as the men amused themselves in the library by discussing medieval history. After the turkey was stuffed with the chestnuts and smoky saucisson we saundered forth to buy the fish. Here is the menu for Christmas Eve dinner from a simple bourgeois household in 1968:

Caviar and Champagne

Oysters on the half shell

Poached salmon

Foie Gras

Turkey stuffed with chestnuts, sausage

Brussel Sprouts

Roast Potatoes (in a clay pot rubbed with garlic and baked)

Green Salad

Nuts, Port, Camembert,

Rhum au baba

There were grand Bordeaux and even better Burgundies, both red and white, brother-in-law Bernard being a *marchand de vin*. With his shiny pencil moustache and more than a soupcon of innuendo his silver boar cutlery stand mounted my silver rabbit, time and again. We sat down at 9 P.M. and rose from the table at 3 A.M. I have no idea what we talked about but it is as if all were one around that table, twelve people as a single organism, laughter and smoke and fumes and a joie de vivre that made life in England intolerable for the six months after. This was historically the first of the feasts before Spring plantings and having to endure the long cold and dark European winters. Lee said that peasants in past centuries sat around drinking spirits for a couple of months in winter with their only chores keeping the animals fed.

Alain and Michelle came for a reciprocal visit to Lancaster, from their little house, bright and warm on a winding medieval street, to Newlands Road our new house in a new project a few feet from the M6 . . . . during the rainy season. We gave up the master bedroom, arranged outings, but they were beyond consolation, moody, unhappy being away from home for the first time, waiting for the rain or drizzle let up, then realizing it would not. With sunken hearts and an air of going into battle, Alain threw back a shot of whiskey and gulped a raw egg in red wine, and piled into the car for the drive to Morecambe with its black gooey mud, rotting boardwalk, little ponies, watery ice cream and small portions.

In one of its white table cloth fish houses we ordered plaice, or was it cod, but alors it did not taste fresh, and there was so little that they each ordered it again. The devilled ham pate was trop grasseuse, the vin undrinkable, the bread like wooly sheep, the chicken tasted like fish, (they were in fact fed on fish meal) the Stilton not Roquefort, and how long had we kept that olive oil? And why was the garlic so anemic? The friendship never really recovered though we visited them once more in St. Max when Michelle and I spent three hours a day shopping for food and two hours cooking it and two hours eating it. The tensions from the Lancaster visit were still bristling and cultural resentment bubbling, the coup de grace coming during a TV rerun of *The Sons of Katie Elder* with a fluent French speaking John Wayne. In the heated room after several thousand calories we got uncontrollable giggles about the right wing *fou qui manque une pneumone*. Alain went berserk and ordered us out! After all he was a patriot! He was more American than we were! And Sacre Bleu he supported this Vietnam War because after all France knew what a salaud Ho Chi Minh was. We never saw them again, such is the fragility of what we call friendship.

GALINA IN LONDON

Galina Stovickova joined former ambassador Sir Cecil Parrott's Czech Studies program at the Comenius Center in Lancaster and we always joked that she was a KGB agent sent to spy on him. We later revised that since she had her loving eye on quiet Russian scholar (now at Stanford) David Holloway her leeeetle Russian boy whom she pursued with a Baroque passion, breaking into his bedroom and placing scented nightgowns under his pillow. She was born in Gorky in 1940 and moved to Prague when she married a nephew of Dubcek, the long-suffering Slava. A parody of the Russian personality, wildly swinging from ecstatic elation to the deepest despair, high laughter or downright sobbing, we nevertheless became friends because the idea of a thrill in Lancaster was to have someone to dinner *from another department*.

When she returned from frequent trips to Gorky, Galina always brought huge suitcases of rough and ready vodka which we were invited to shoot back with fried, battered salami, salami wrapped around pickles, cheese and salami canapés and fried pickles. In return for this hospitality she dropped hints at how she would love to own a champagne bucket or a piece of Wedgwood or Waterford, a ploy that always worked because she threw her arms around Lee and kissed him. One day Galina suggested she and I go to London to meet her husband and a friend so we took the bus three long hours down the M6 with a bottle of plum vodka.

Slava and Frantisek Novy, the Czech Minister of Shipping, (I always thought it landlocked) were staying in a small room in a Chelsea hotel where they entertained us sitting on suitcases drinking vodka, and eating salami, cheese and bread. So that was supposed to be dinner? I suggested a visit to the Tower of London! Up they stood from the suitcases, rolled the vodka and the salami under the bed and each slung a large camera over his shoulders. Several hours of snapping this and snapping that, parks and monuments and museums and Hampton Court thence to a pub to change the film. What film? They had none in the cameras! I remembered Petrovich's classes in Madison, and Russian history suddenly became clear!

WINTER IN WINCHESTER

About 6:00 on a black stormy February night we arrived in Winchester. The streets were rain lashed and empty as a robbed tomb. Nothing was open; shutters were shuttered, locks were locked. I looked at the tiny car and thought I could not endure another night such as the one in Arles, sleeping on the Plaza. Ah ha. A light in yonder window. We knock on a door. A fat man with a fag in his mouth, a soiled undershirt and half beard said yes there was a room for the night and yes his name was Will Shakespeare. No relation.

The room was 'just vacated' and indeed it was-just-with dirty towels in the bathroom, a half made bed on which we reclined fully dressed outside the sheets, an unused condom on the bedstead. Then-dinner. Will had some dandy steak, which after dropping on the floor he wiped off on his pants and slapped on the plates. It was what I imagined a Turkish prison to be like. But that was not all. Will was lonely and brought out a bottle of whisky and proceeded to tell us about the Roman helmets and Roman things galore which he had just found in the passageway under the house leading to the Cathedral, and would we like to go down into the bowels of the house and see them in the tunnel? Lee said yes and I said no, thinking of recent hideous murders in dark streets in Manchester and other places in his black forbidding decidedly—not—Cambridge land. Well we did not go into the tunnel but did tell Lawrence Stone about it and a year after it was announced in the papers that a cache of Roman ruins had been found in the passageway between Shakespeare's Inn and Winchester Cathedral.

The next morning skipping breakfast we absconded and found a B & B, a Mrs. Jackson's down the road a bit. We could not avoid English breakfasts while travelling the land to haunt county record offices and graveyards and church vaults for evidence of those sturdy beggars. A whole day in a damp room with those abominable microfiche machines reading impenetrable curlicue Elizabethan script usually necessitated a fuel burning breakfast, but since we had that every morning for a week we suggested to tiny spry Mrs. Jackson that we would love something a little different for breakfast.

Thawed out from the lone blanket and huddling together in sweaters and gloves we were the sole breakfasters at the table. In walked our hostess with a broad smile informing us of a special treat—kippers! Two each and there was more in the kitchen. Now kippers are great in the evening mixed with a little butter and dill and spread on a cracker or in kedgeree when there was no haddock available, but for breakfast! In a freezing house! Out she went leaving us alone with four artificially smoked bright orange herring. As luck would have it we saw a cat the same color as the kippers, a fat fellow who sat nonchalantly under the table perhaps accustomed to all of this, so piece by piece we fed him the treats until Mrs. Jackson returned to clear the plates. "Timmy, Timmy this is for you love." Timmy was inert on the floor. Shaking her head Mrs. Jackson was totally baffled and could not understand why the ginger tom did not want kippers. Oh well perhaps he was ill and there was a vet she would have to take him to see.

AFRICA NORTH AND SOUTH

Dinner with Mike and Jane Egan was usually a roast chicken in their tiny cottage but one night we all went to that Indian restaurant where we had discovered Glass in the Curry. Mike was from South Africa, Jewish, about 5'4" tall, and with enough vitality and humor and sass as I ever was to witness in my entire life. In walked two strapping Lancashiremen. One was his landlord who snarled that Mike owed him rent (well he should have sold those real Moore bronzes on the mantelpiece) and called him a little Jew Bastard. Up stood all 6'4" of Lee Beier with that mean glint in his beady eyes (when threatened with firing at the university he said he would shoot the professors and he looked like he really meant it) and the landlord retreated. We feared for Mike's life though the English are verbally vicious and rarely took to their fists, but during these years I witnessed not only blatant anti Semitism but profound anti foreigner feeling, as with those Paki Bashin navvies in Preston. This would all erupt in 1981 but for the time being everyone blamed Enoch Powell for inviting the golliwogs in to man the service industries.

South Africa was strictly infra dig; we closed our Barclay's account when we learned it still supported apartheid. Mike's friend, a student leader in Johannesburg, Adrian Leftwich who was the subject of Christopher Driver's *Elegy for a Revolutionary* spent several years in Lancaster after having been tortured in prison in South Africa and the fact that his ideas were actually translated into action made him a hero. I wanted to be especially gracious so decided to cook bobotie, which is probably the last thing he wanted to eat. It is a lamb or beef curry with apricots and béchamel custard on top, a kind of Afrikkaner version of moussaka. It still ranks as one of my favorite dishes in the world!

When it came to cooking Ruth and Abe Sirton (who was a freedom fighter in Yugoslavia under Tito) had me under their spell. They entertained weekly, always a fascinating, decidedly not homogeneous group. At their weekly dinners we met the international set who were usually studying business administration at the University, as well as several friends of the Sirtons from their long sojurn teaching in Ghana. There was English Lit. student Adeph from Egypt who made a miraculous pork and prune stew, Aurora Fernandez a devoted child of Castro's Cuba and now the minister of Education. There were anti Shah Iranians galore and Communists from Brooklyn.

My own interest in politics, global or otherwise, was not extensive so I talked to Ruthie about the correct way to make the borscht simmering in the most gigantic pot I had ever seen sit atop a stove. When the sour cream was added I was in an aesthetic heaven the color was so exquisite. Her chicken stew from Ghana was the first time I tasted peanuts in a main dish and it was out of this world. No one was ever alone if the Sirtons could help it. They became my social world as I dropped out of all the consciousness—raising groups and women's encounter groups where everyone criticized each other in the name of honesty, and the peculiar left wing sects and all the revolutionary plotting, all of which came to nothing. Far better to eat borscht and sing Avanti Populo.

Walking the Hills, Dales and Moors

We hiked on the weekends with John King or with Mick Murray the "mature" (i.e. a bit older) student leader and ardent Communist, and his friend old Red Max Adereth. Once or twice, mainly because I had a crush on Mick, I attended Communist party meetings in Morecambe and noted in my journals that "the world has nothing to fear from this rag tag group of ancient losers". University campuses were rife with dissidents and some might say oddballs such as Max or Mick or Dave, AKA Carol, Riddell who underwent a sex change operation from male to female so (s)he could become a radical feminist.

The Pennine Way, the high fells of the Lake District and the Yorkshire moors were the great levelers of all sects and classes since everyone walked and hiked and scrambled at every opportunity, everyone who was English that is, and us. We bought sturdy and expensive hiking boots from Switzerland which we religiously cared for with dousings of mink oil which ended up rotting the laces and not waterproofing them at all. Americans and those from the Continent rarely if ever took part in this arduous, uncomfortable sport and in a way you can see why not. You cannot imagine mortal terror until you have walked on high peaks in the dark with high winds swirling and the temperature dropping rapidly and nothing to guide you, risking death by hypothermia on the hostile, very narrow foggy ridges. Bill Bryson accurately captures the menace and madness of fell climbing, "ambling on sheer faced crags clattering over scree, towering citadels or rocks into 'a cold, bleak netherworld so remote and forbidding that even the sheep seemed startled to see us'.

Hartsopp Dodd was just such a cold, bleak netherworld, a sinister high ridge on a particularly sinister stretch of the fells, where we ascended early one somewhat sunny morning, meaning we could see a bit of blue between the looming clouds. We parked the car at the bottom of the hill and merrily set off with my brother, visiting from New York. The first hundred yards were all green, grassy slopes and good cheer, then the clouds became a little heavier and the grassy hill turned to dangerous scree, the loose slate left behind after the mines closed. At Lee's Germanic insistence up and up we went for hours with our Wainwright and Ordnance Survey map furiously flapping in the screaming wind as ice shards cut into our hands and faces.

It grew darker and darker and uglier and uglier until, absolutely freezing, we could see no more as we vainly searched for three bloody cairns Lee insisted were to lead the way to the top of the ridge. No luck. Donny, who had never been on top of a treacherous mountain, was in tears and I was as furious as the wind. Then I spied a stone fence descending down the hellish height. Lee yelled that we'd fall off if we took that route down, but clinging to every rock we inched our way, past sheep skulls and slippery stones in the black fog and pure indescribable terror as Lee trudged upwards.

After awhile we saw a light, a faint yellow light, and followed in the direction, still descending perilously, the stone fence having abruptly ended in the middle of nowhere. Then a pub! A bloody pub! The sky was pitch black that frightful night but the room had a blazing fireplace and we sat and had a pint as we tried to figure out how to get back to the car should Lee never return, which he did a half hour later full of scorn for our cowardice. We ate pasties and drank bitters and forgot the terror but

I never went on a hill again with Lee. After Donny's death in 2002 I threw away the sheep skull we had brought home with us from Hartsop Dodd that terrifying day.

POCHEEN

The Irish were still treated like unwanted invaders in this part of the country where Roman Catholicism had flourished since the 17th century. The Irish lads and lasses I taught at Our Lady's were sad, skinny waifs. When one summer we returned to America the blacks seemed so prosperous compared to these medieval ragamuffins whose heads were regularly bashed on desks or who were periodically flogged in the headmaster's office. They expected capital punishment and often dared me to hit them, which I never did, so they rioted in the classroom, making my departure inevitable. "Mrs. Beier, you MUST establish order in your classroom!" bleated Mr. Conroy the head master whose main interest was bending down picking up scraps of paper recalcitrant students dropped en route to forced readings of *Wind in the Willows*.

David Holloway was Irish, only the *other* Ireland of Trinity College and the professions. Before he married Arlene the Glaswegian newscaster we visited his bachelor self many times at the University of Edinburgh where haggis and bagpipes were always dragged out if they heard an American accent. We often ate the chieftain o' the puddin race on our visits, and I tried not to think of lungs and hearts and other parts of dead sheep mixed with oatmeal, onions, tons of black pepper boiled in casings that were supposed to be a sheep's stomach. After splitting it open, when it was still steaming hot, we always added a shot of, say, Glen Morange and ate it lustily with tart, sour white turnips. It was served on January 25th Burn's night for visitors only since our group was too scornful of such kitsch activities.

One night David threw a haggis dinner for the Dooley's from Dublin and it was my first exposure to pocheen a sort of eau de vie made from fermented potatoes. Irish drinking of alcoholic beverages is strictly a cultural phenomenon and not a genetic disease we consider it in Puritan America. It's simply what they did and what they do! Pocheen possessed none of the aromatics of mirabelle but was as raw and unpalatable as grappa, as harsh as the land itself, but whatever the potion I loved nothing more than fraternizing and drinking around a dinner table, surely one of the ways the gods permitted us to deal with the Truths of Life. Besides when you think of Irish history and the abominable oppression since Elizabethan times you can understand why numbing the mind and senses was essential to Irish survival. In the 20th century it had simply become a cultural habit that connected one with the spirits of one's ancestors.

PRINCE CHARLES'S
ECO-GASTRONOMY

The folks up North could not have given another tu'penny damn about Prince Charles or the rest of the Royals, but he always had a place in my affections since his earnestness and studiousness reminded me of the young, idealistic Lee I had married. I have always felt Charles would have been a great Cambridge don with rather obscure intellectual interests—the more obscure the better. When, many years after I left England, the *New York Times* reported that the "Prince's Technology Qualms Create a Stir in Britain", I knew what was in store, veiled sarcasm and a politically correct attitude about the infallibility of progress, a myth I had long ago discarded. Prince Charles, concerned about nanotechnology and its godlike manipulation of subatomic molecules, asked the Royal Society if research were being sufficiently regulated. After all, artificially created nanoparticles *had* appeared intermixed with living cells in the organs of research animals and then there was that mercenary behavior of those who profited (including recent convicted felons) from biotech companies.

The broad humanist education he received at Cambridge, always noted for its scientific prowess, has always been a wedge between him ordinary folk as it was between him and a myopic media. An average student at Trinity, his moral tutor Kitson-Clark once told Lee the Prince was "a very good note taker"; he was the first heir to the throne to attend school, complete a university education, then try to put it to some use. To choose to live the life of an 18th century gentleman farmer which was every Englishman's dream before the pathetic lionization of soccer stars, is not merely an anthropological curiosity but actually of some urgent importance.

Charles has not only practiced organic farming but has questioned the safety of genetically engineered crops as well as 'advanced' farming methods which indisputably created hoof and mouth and mad cow disease via cross-species breeding. Cumbria was the hardest hit of all the counties in the 2001 outbreak of hoof and mouth and after most of the sheep were slaughtered the new generation had to relearn heaf-ing or returning to their turf. Regarding mixing molecules around, I for one can no longer eat a BLT without knowing that the tomato has the DNA of a flounder, the lettuce is actually a poppy plant that underwent radiation, the bacon made from chemistry-lab, tortured animals, the bread, the mayo . . . well it is clear! One only wishes Charles had questioned the use of artificial hormones in women since it might have saved countless lives.

His quasi-socialistic ideas derive from the optimistic romanticism, with a touch of positivism, of the late 19th century, from William Morris, John Ruskin and Roger Fry's mentor, Edward Carpenter, a time when it was believed that the human condition could be improved by nurture as well as nature. The model village of Poundbury designed by Leon Krier with Charles' significant input and embodying the principles of the "return of human values to architecture" employs traditional materials, negotiable scale and local vernacular styles as harmonious blending with the landscape. In 1984 on the 150th anniversary of the Royal Academy of Architecture at a lecture in Hampton Court Palace, Charles referred to the proposed National Gallery extension on the South Bank of the Thames as "a monstrous carbuncle on the face of a much-loved and elegant friend." a metaphor that has done its duty as a synonym for Carolingian reaction. It is actually not only, to this art historian, a very funny but very accurate description of the ghastly creations of "New Brutalist" architects; equally funny and accurate is his description of the British Museum's new Reading

Room as "an assembly hall of an academy for secret police." These ideas are cut from the same cloth as the reaction to genetic engineering. *Ainsi-soit-il.*

Certainly it is far easier to speculate on the possibility of human happiness if you are unconscionably privileged but he is nonetheless in tune with the science of the natural universe. Like so many of the professors and lecturers I knew he has large ideas in an age when ideology is dead such as Julian Huxley, Buckminster Fuller, and Laurens van der Post, the godfather of his son, William. You have to love a man who could say, "I am apparently accused of having dangerously old fashioned views of just about everything. But, by God, I am proud to be old fashioned if it means minding about local identity, about food made by hand."

Charles is a driving force behind the Slow Food movement to which I feel morally obliged to belong; in a speech at the Terra Madre 2004 Conference in Milan he mentioned Ruskin, so dear to this heart, but more importantly reiterated his commitment to small-scale agriculture, artisanal food production and the holistic philosophy of sustainability. Whether this is practical remains to be seen but I do know Prince Charles annually visits the farmers and sheepherders of Cumbria and North Lancashire, and supports local food traditions in that part of the green island that has suffered most the depredations of modern agricultural practices and the Industrial Revolution.

Almost a century after Roger Fry made his reference to *Bird's Custard Island,* Jane Grigson had a few words to say about its dubious heritage, "Another blow has been the commercialization of puddings premixed in packets, with skimmed milk powder, chemical flavor, chemical color and chemical preservation. Custard powder made in this way has been one of our minor national tragedies."

Some Recipes From The Northwest

Lancashire, North and South, abounds with old family recipes such as Preston Gingerbread, Wet Nellie, Morecambe Bay Potted Shrimp, Hindle Wakes Chicken, Pea Whack, Sad Cakes from Lumb-in-Rossendale, Hotpot and Lobscouse. Until recently suet appeared in just about everything from sweet cakes to meat stews, and sugar, rum and dried fruits were ubiquitous. This was also the case in Cumbria where regional delicacies included damson plums, lake char, exotic spices and a peppercake from Appleby where gypsies congregate every summer for horse racing, merry making and the occasional fist fight. Here is a small selection of recipes readers should try for something a bit out of the ordinary.

Coniston Cheesecake

Pulse in a food processor 8 ounces of curd or finely sieved cottage cheese, 4 eggs, 1 ounce ground almonds, 5 ounces currants, 2 ounces heavy cream, 2 ounces butter, 8 ounces sugar, grated lemon zest,1 teaspoon nutmeg, glass of sherry or brandy.

Pour in pastry lined pan with pastry lattice pastry strips on top

Bake for 30 minutes

Cumberland Rum Butter

This was served to visitors with Havver bread when a newborn baby
   arrived.

It is also fine with Christmas pudding and gingerbread.

Cream together 8 ounces butter, 6 ounces brown sugar, 5 ounces of rum

Grate a good sprinkle of nutmeg into the butter and refrigerate.

Cumberland Sauce

Grate the rinds of 1 orange and 1 lemon

Simmer zest and the juice of the fruits with 6 ounces red currant jelly till
   dissolved

Add 1 tablespoon prepared mustard, 4 tablespoons port, and a grating of
   ginger

Boil and reduce by half.

If using this with venison or lamb add a cinnamon stick to the above.

Damson Gin

Mash 2 pounds of plums removing pits

Add 1 pound or more of granulated sugar till dissolved

Add 4 pints of gin and let sit in dark place about a month or two—if possible.

Damson Jam

Simmer 2 pounds damson plums, 2 pounds sugar, 1/2 pint water and the
   juice of a lemon until it begins to thicken.

You'll know when it's about ready since it has natural pectin and will start
   to thicken. Cool and enjoy it with toast and tea.

Derwentwater Duckling

Stick 4 cloves into 4 small onions

Place inside duck and **roast** 1 hour, basting

Turn duck upside down and roast ½ hour

Pour off fat and add ½ pint stock, 1 ounce flour, 4 tablespoons Cumberland
Sauce and 3 tablespoons of brandy

Carve duck and serve with sauce

Easter Ledge Pudding

Soak 2 tablespoons of barley in water overnight

Simmer in water a handful of nettles, bistorts or any herbs with 1 small
chopped cabbage, 2 sliced leeks and 1 chopped onion for about 25
minutes, then drain well.

Add 2 or 3 eggs, the drained barley, 3 tablespoons of butter, black
pepper

Place in casserole dish and bake 15 minutes or fry as patties in butter

Hasty Pudding

This is Dorothy Wordsworth's recipe which she probably made for her
brother William. It reminds me of my undergraduate staple supper
dish.

Mix 8 ounces oatmeal, 2 ½ cups milk, 1 egg yolk, 2 ounces brown sugar, a
dot of butter and pinch of salt

Simmer for a few minutes

Havver Bread

Hafrar is the Old Norse word for oats. This is also great with cheese and pate.

Mix together 6 ounces of oatmeal, 2 ounces of whole wheat flour, a pinch of salt and a teaspoon of baking soda.

Add the mixture to a tablespoon of any fatty drippings, including bacon or vegetable oil, then add enough boiling water to make a thick paste.

Roll out to 1/2 inch thick and cut into triangles

Bake 25 minutes

Herb Tart

Mix together 1/2 cup light cream, 1 ounce of breadcrumbs, 2 packages thawed and drained spinach (or that handful of wild herbs), 2 crumbled macaroons, some currants, a bit of melted butter, 3 eggs and a tablespoon or two of sugar.

Put mixture in a shell of prepared puff pastry and **bake** at 325 until filling sets.

Hunter's Pot

Marinate 2 or 3 pounds of cubed venison or stewing steak overnight in red wine, juniper berries and bayleaf.

Fry 2 onions and add marinade along with shallot, garlic, a spoon tomato paste, bouquet garni.

Add the marinated meat and cover with the marinade and stock to cover

Cook 2-3 hours in a medium oven and right before end add 2 tablespoons of red currant jelly.

Serve with herbed biscuits.

Kunwar's Curry

Mix together 1 teaspoon turmeric, ½ teaspoon chili pepper, ½ teaspoon coriander, 1/2 of ginger, ¼ teaspoon cumin, salt and black pepper.

Make a paste of the spices sautéed in ghee or clarified butter, to which fried onions and one clove of garlic and plain yoghurt are added. To this is added skinless chicken, sautéed for a few minutes, then covered with water and simmered for an hour. At the last minute add a big pinch of Garam Masala and serve with

Basmati Rice which is fried first in a bit of ghee then never touched; add ½ inch of boiling water above the rice, place a cloth place in lid and cover tightly, steaming off the heat, for 20 minutes. A nice golden crust forms on bottom of rice. Highly prized.

Serve with lime pickle, Gray's Mango Chutney

Lancashire Hindle Wakes

Because this recipe has so many ingredients I am going to use the traditional listing format

The chicken:

1 large chicken
2 cups soaked prunes with kernels
1 tablespoon mixed herbs
pinch of mace and cinnamon
a cup breadcrumbs
juice 1 lemon
1 tablespoon vegetable oil or suet

1 large onion

4 ounces malt vinegar

10 ounces chicken stock

1 ounce brown sugar

The sauce:

1 ounce butter

2 ounces milk

juice and grated rind of lemon

1 ounce flour

¼ pint heavy cream

Stuff the bird with prunes, breadcrumbs, oil, herbs, spices, lemon juice. Cover with stock and 4 ounces of malt vinegar and 1 ounce of brown sugar. Simmer very slowly 2 to 3 hours. Drain and make the sauce with the classic béchamel style adding lemon juice and cream towards the end. Coat the chicken with the sauce and sprinkle with grated lemon rind and halved prunes. Serve cold.

Lancashire Hotpot

Sauté 1 pound floured lamb shoulder cubes or lamb steaks in butter till brown

Add 2 lamb kidneys and a black pudding chopped (optional)

Saute 2 large onions till browned

Layer 1 large sliced potato in a buttered casserole

Add meat(s) sprinkled with ½ teaspoon of thyme, a pinch of mace and 1 teaspoon of brown sugar

Layer onions and 3 more sliced potatoes, which should be last layer

Pour 1 pint of stock over all

Put butter pats on top

Bake covered for 2 hours. In the last hour remove lid to brown potatoes

Parkin

Mix together 16 ounces oatmeal, 8 ounces flour, 1 teaspoon baking soda

Melt 8 ounces of butter and add 16 ounces molasses or treacle

Add to dry ingredients and stir with some milk until soft

Bake at 325 in greased square pan for 90 minutes and let rest for 24 hours

Penrith Spiced Pepper

Combine 1 ounce each white pepper, ground mace, nutmeg, add ½ ounce
    cayenne. Seasons any meat dish to perfection.

Pork with Oranges

Fry one pound of cubed pork till brown

Saute 1 sliced onion and 1 sliced orange

Add ½ pink of hard cider, a pinch of sage

Simmer covered for 30 minutes

Thicken with 1 tablespoon flour and 2 tablespoons marmalade.

Potted Char

Simmer 6 ounce piece of char, salmon or trout, 1 small onion, a carrot,
    chopped parsley and ½ glass of white wine with enough water to cover

Drain and place in a small earthenware dish

Pour 8 ounces melted butter over the fish

Bake for 20 minutes.

Place thin layer of clarified butter over cooled fish

Potted Cheese

Pulse any hard dried cheese in food processor

Add half as much butter and some dry sherry to processor and blend

Put in crockery pots

Potted Salmon

Cream together 1 pound chopped smoked Scottish salmon, ¼ pint heavy cream,

Add a pinch each of salt, some cayenne, mace and a squeeze anchovy paste.

Pour 3 ounces clarified butter over top

Chill overnight

Potted Shrimp

Buy 1 pound of small shrimp, preferably from Morecambe Bay

Melt 4 ounces butter

Add a pinch each of mace, nutmeg and cayenne

Cover with a layer of clarified butter

Place in small ramekins and refrigerate

Rum Dog

Soak some raisins in rum

Mix with flour and suet and water

Make a stiff dough and add the drained raisins

Steam in buttered pudding basin

Feed to the hungry hounds—and yourselves if any left over.

Kendal Steak and Kidney Pudding

Of course this is universal in all Britannia but the North prided itself on its fine version and who can resist adding it here?

Brown in butter 2 pounds rump or stewing steak and 1 lamb or ox kidney (optional)

Brown 1 onion in same pot after meat removed

Add flour, 1 pint of good stock, tomato paste or wine

Simmer 2 hours

Add 8 ounces of chopped mushrooms

Place in suet crust in buttered pudding basin

Add a suet crust on top and steam for 1-2 hours

Sheep Herders Fattie Cake

You don't get more authentic than this.

Mix 10 ounces of flour with 4 ounces of suet and 1 ½ ounces of lard.

Proof yeast ½ ounce in warm milk

Mix together with pinch of salt

Let rise then **Shape** into 5 small loaves

Bake 10 minutes

Skipton Tonic

Skipton is right over the border in Yorkshire but this is too interesting to
leave out.

Mix together some orange peel, Chamomile leaves, grated ginger

Warm a good amount of brandy and pour over the above.

Let sit for a day or two before drinking.

Tatie Pot

Saute 1 pound of cubed lamb, 1 pound beef shin, and a sliced black pudding

Add 6 tablespoons of barley, 2 pounds potatoes and two sliced onions

Add stock to cover and simmer 2 hours

Westmorland Lamb Pie

Mix together ½ cup each of the following: currants, raisins, sultanas, citrus peel

Add 1 pound cooked lamb cut in small pieces, 2 peeled and grated apples,
1/4 pint water or orange juice, 8 ounces brown sugar, 4-6 ounces dark
rum, 2 ounces chopped almonds and a pinch each of mace, nutmeg,
cinnamon

Place in shortcrust pastry on the top and bottom, brushed with egg wash
and bake 30-45 minutes at 400F.

Westmorland Pepper Cake

Mix 16 ounces flour and 1 teaspoon baking powder

Rub in 4 ounces butter

Beat 2 eggs with 8 ounces treacle or molasses

Add 8 ounces fried fruit, 1/4 pound granulated sugar

Add ½ teaspoon each ground ginger and powdered cloves, and black pepper

Mix together and bake 1 hour

Windermere Spiced Biscuits

Mix together 12 ounces self rising flour, 8 ounces butter, 8 ounces brown sugar, 2 teaspoons caraway seeds, 1 teaspoon cinnamon, 2 eggs

Knead into a nice soft dough

Roll ½ inch thick and cut into cookies

Bake for 20 minutes